TRIUMPH
BOOKS

THE ROAD TO
TEXAS

THE ROAD TO
TEXAS

Incredible Twists and Improbable Turns
Along the Longhorns Recruiting Trail

Mike Roach

TRIUMPH
B O O K S

Library of Congress Cataloging-in-Publication Data available upon request

This book is available in quantity at special discounts for your group or organization. For further information, contact:

Triumph Books LLC
814 North Franklin Street
Chicago, Illinois 60610
(312) 337-0747
www.triumphbooks.com

Printed in U.S.A.
ISBN: 978-1-63727-109-4
Design by Patricia Frey
Photos courtesy of AP Images

*To my wife, Kylie, for her belief and unwavering
support of me and my career.*

To my friends and family who inspire and motivate me every day.

To my father, Greg, who first instilled in me a love for football.

*To my grandfather Del, who passed when I was 15 years
old but still holds such a powerful influence in my life.*

Contents

Foreword

There have been many events that have shaped my life, both as an individual and as a broadcaster of Texas Longhorns football, basketball, and baseball games for more than 30 years and of Texas high school sports for more than 40 years. But there are two dates that will always stand out as reasons for me discovering my life's professional calling. They exemplify the spectacle and the way of life that is football in Texas.

On December 6, 1969, I was a nine-year-old growing up in North Carolina. I just happened to walk into the living room of my parents' house that afternoon and my uncle, who was a native of Pottsville, Texas, had the ABC telecast of the Texas-Arkansas game on. I sat down, curious about this team with the Longhorn on their helmets playing this other team with the snarling pig on the side of their helmets. It was the first time I had even heard the name Razorbacks.

My uncle pointed out the coach on the Texas sideline and said, "That's the great Darrell Royal," and told me that this was the battle between the No. 1 and 2 teams in the nation. I was glued to the telecast. I watched the entire game (something I had not done much of in my early days), and when the Longhorns had escaped Fayetteville with a 15–14 victory, with a national championship plaque presented to the team in the locker room from President Nixon and their No. 1 final ranking secured, I was "hooked" as a Texas Longhorns fan.

I continued to follow Texas throughout my teen years, and when I moved to Texas in 1978, I was still a Longhorns fan. I was a sophomore attending North Lake College in Irving, Texas. A journalism student, I had picked up a part-time job at the *Carrollton Times Chronicle*, a suburban newspaper north of Dallas. My assignment was to cover a couple of the area's high school football teams, and the first Texas high school football game I ever saw was a season opener on September 5, 1980, between W.T. White High School of Dallas (the Longhorns, by the way) and the Lake Highlands Wildcats, also a school located within the Dallas city limits, but actually part of the Richardson school district. While I had covered my high school's football team for the school newspaper back in North Carolina, I was totally unprepared for what Texas high school football was all about— the size of the bands, the cheerleaders, drill teams, pristine artificial turf field, and 12,000-plus fans in the stands—and I was mesmerized.

I became addicted to Texas high school football that night. I began to read about all of the top teams in the state, the history of the game, the five classifications of 11-man football, what this strange six-man version of the game was also like, as well as the playoff structure, with postseason games played in collegiate and professional sports stadiums in front of tens of thousands of fans.

By the time I had finished college in the mid-1980s, I had managed to talk the station manager at KNTU, the student-run radio station at the University of North Texas, into carrying weekly live high school football broadcasts. It was on these broadcasts of Pilot Point Bearcats and Lewisville Fighting Farmers football games that I honed my play-by-play skills and strengthened my love for all things Texas high school football. My first radio broadcast job at KRLD in Dallas in the mid-'80s allowed me to expand my horizons, first as a 10-year host of a high school football Friday night scoreboard show that many were able to hear because of the station's 50,000-watt nighttime signal, then as a play-by-play broadcaster when we added the KRLD High School Football Game of the Week in the late '80s.

I had also begun to see what recruiting was all about, including the almost lawless manner in which some schools would stop at almost nothing to secure the services of a top-flight running back, quarterback, or linebacker. Through it all, I remained a Texas Longhorns fan—although I had to cloak my fandom in secrecy when I secured the studio anchor position on the Southwest Conference Radio Network in 1988. I was the studio anchor for all nine Southwest Conference schools' broadcasts at that time (Arkansas was still in the SWC back then), so I would stifle my enthusiasm for a Texas victory when recapping a Longhorns' win over another team from the league.

Two more significant developments arrived in 1992. I began hosting a weekly television show on what was then known as HSE (Home Sports Entertainment), later known as Prime Sports, then Fox Sports Southwest, and most recently Bally Sports Southwest. *High School Xtra* allowed me the opportunity to travel across the state of Texas, traversing thousands of miles over the next seven years doing features and interviews with hundreds of players, coaches, and fans, as well as with officials from the University Interscholastic League, the governing body of Texas high school athletics. I was able to see firsthand the passion, the investment, and the way of life that is high school football for people in cities as large as Houston and as small as Celina, traveling from Texarkana to El Paso, up to Amarillo, down to the Rio Grande Valley, and to all points in between. It was also here that I witnessed the heartbeat of the game—the student-athlete and future recruit. This show would eventually grow into *High School Scoreboard Live*, which I have hosted on the network for more than 25 years.

That 1992 season also delivered my debut on the Texas Longhorns Radio Network as an analyst for Longhorns football and men's basketball games, working alongside play-by-play voice Bill Schoening. When Bill left the position in the fall of 2001 to become the San Antonio Spurs play-by-play voice, I moved into my dream job: play-by-play voice of the Texas Longhorns. It is a position I have always treasured and respected, and I have always tried to translate my passion for the Longhorns, and for the game, into each and every broadcast in the more than 20 years I have held this position.

The years of covering and broadcasting high school and college football have allowed me to cross paths with many individuals in the industry. I have encountered varying degrees of interest and investment; some of these folks truly care as much as I do about their craft, and others not nearly as much. But in the many years that I have been around both recruiting from the high school level and the collegiate selection process, I have encountered few individuals with the interest, attention to detail, and passion displayed by Mike Roach.

Reading Mike's articles and visiting with him on the air or in person reassures me that there are indeed those freaky people like me who truly "get it." Those rare individuals invest their time, effort, interest, and passion for the game of football, the high school game, the process that involves the most important decision in a young man's life (at least up to that moment), and also what the process means to college football and to the University of Texas. In this book,

Mike encapsulates the thoughts, feelings, and emotions of those who are centrally involved with the process, and also delivers the scene properly—the exciting and the mundane, the suspenseful and the disappointing. This is a guy who has traveled across Texas and back again just as I have—a man who has eaten more than his share of overcooked eggs and undercooked chicken fried steaks in cafés all across the Lone Star State—and a man who dearly loves his profession and the craftwork necessary to carry it out to top-flight levels.

If you've driven, as I have, long stretches of road in this state—roads such as US-90 Alternate through Lavaca County, State Highway 54 between Van Horn and Guadalupe Peak, or I-30 between Sulphur Springs and Mount Pleasant—know this: Mike Roach has driven them as well, and many thousands of miles more. It is his account of the high school football and recruiting scene along the highways and byways of Texas that makes *The Road to Texas* an entertaining and intriguing read.

—Craig Way, Texas Longhorns Radio Network

CHAPTER I

Derrick Johnson

Derrick Johnson is usually the best athlete in any room he's in. Johnson grew up in Waco, Texas, as part of an athletic family. Johnson's older brother Dwight played at Baylor and went on to have a career in the NFL. His first cousins Bert Emanuel, Kevin Emanuel, Aaron Emanuel, Ben Emanuel, and John Williams all played at the collegiate level.

Johnson himself was an athletic marvel. During his senior year Johnson played outside linebacker at a listed size of 6'3" and 205 pounds. A Parade All-American and two-time All-State selection, the most terrifying thing about Johnson was his elite speed to go with his size.

This product of Waco High School was a three-sport star, playing basketball and running in track-and-field events when he was away from the football field. As a senior, Johnson ran a blistering 10.5-second 100-meter time and triple jumped at 48'. Combine that athletic context with his size and production, and it's easy to see why he was so heavily recruited.

But Johnson never thought about the future. While everyone was lining up to tell him about all the great things he could do after high school, Johnson followed the adage of being where your feet are. Recruiting has changed quite a bit since 2001, when Johnson graduated from high school. Early offers weren't as in vogue as they are now. Even still, it was late in his high school career when Johnson realized he had a future in football.

"It was probably my 11th grade year," Johnson said. "That's kind of late. I've always been a guy that is very low-key and all about my business. I don't listen to the outside noise much. People would always tell me, 'You're going to go to the NFL. You're going to go to college, and you're going to do this and that.' I was always like, 'I'm in high school, and I've got to figure this out right now and be the best that I can be, working on being an All-American and working on being the best linebacker [in] Texas.' That was always my goal. I've done a great job of conquering where I was at during that moment."

Before social media, video conferencing, and text messaging, schools used the postal service to communicate interest with prospective student-athletes. Johnson started to get a few letters during his sophomore season, but contact picked up during his junior year when the power programs in the region started to reach out.

"I got so many letters," Johnson said. "My 10th grade year I got a couple letters here and there. There were a couple of small schools, and then 11th grade came up. It was when everyone started sending letters. And, honestly, I can't remember the [first] school, but I do remember the ones that always stuck out to me. The OU, the Texas, the Texas A&M. You know those Texas schools; those were always going to be at the top of my list. And I remember those more."

Johnson grew up in the shadow of Baylor University. Waco High School stands less than five miles west of the Baylor campus across I-35. Johnson grew up watching the Bears, and his older brother

Dwight suited up for Baylor from 1996 to 1999. Johnson spent plenty of time at Floyd Casey Stadium watching the Bears and was an ardent fan of the Green and Gold.

Still he always had an eye on Austin. It didn't hurt that several Waco residents ended up in Austin and made a name for themselves. It also didn't hurt that Baylor was struggling as a football program at the time. While his brother was on campus, Baylor was 16–39 as a program. During the final three years of that run, Baylor won a total of just five games.

"I always liked Texas," Johnson said. "My love for them grew, but I was a Baylor fan. Living in Waco, and my brother played for Baylor, so I went to all the games—and during '95 to '99 they lost a lot. So I saw a lot during that time, but I was a big-time Baylor fan because my brother played for them. My sister went there and graduated from there, so when you talk about, you know, 'Sic 'em Bears,' I was doing that. During my high school days I've always had my eye on Texas. Kwame Cavil—he's from Waco. He played at Waco High. So that was a guy I'm like, 'Oh, okay, that, that helps me to get more gravitated to Texas.' Obviously watching Ricky Williams and those guys—Wane McGarity, Shaun Rogers, and Casey Hampton [Jr.]—and those guys like Quentin Jammer. I mean, you can name all—I'm watching these guys. Now I was more of a Baylor guy, but Texas, obviously, was beating Baylor. It grew on me more and more, and I was like, 'Man, I've got to have that Longhorn on the side of my helmet in college.' That Longhorn symbol, regardless of where you are in Texas, you know that symbol. You know what it stands for. You know the richness and tradition of Texas. Even if you don't want to go there, you know it."

While Johnson watched his brother on the field for Baylor, a Bears assistant coach was on the field coaching who would one day lead the elite linebacker to Texas. Darryl Drake served one year at Baylor as offensive coordinator and quarterback coach. After leaving Waco following a two-win season, Drake was hired by Mack Brown on his initial staff at Texas. Drake served as the wide receivers coach in Austin, but his year in Waco allowed him to build a relationship with Johnson's family through Johnson's older brother.

When Texas began to recruit Johnson, Drake was the obvious candidate for the task. Relationships are often the most important component of getting an athlete to a school. Drake's bond with the family was so strong that Mack Brown took a hands-off approach. Brown was usually heavily involved in the recruitments of his players, but, while he kept in contact, he let Drake do the heavy lifting.

"He was a good friend of ours," Johnson said. "He was at Baylor. So they did a smart thing. When he was at Baylor he knew my brother. After my brother left, he left too, and he went to Texas. Obviously, because of that connection, Coach Brown put him on me. Mack Brown didn't even come sit in my house. You know, some coaches, you see them make the rounds. I talked to him all the time on the phone, so he wasn't distant like that. When it comes to knowing who's going to relate to certain people—and who already knows the families like Coach Drake did? You go down there, you go talk to him. I was very impressed. My mom was impressed because we didn't talk much about football. It was more talking about academics and family. Just making sure that my mom felt secure in sending her young son to Austin. Drake did a great job."

Drake's involvement didn't mean that Brown completely stayed out of it. In the 2000s nobody worked a room and enchanted parents of a recruit like the Texas head coach. In fact Brown did so well with Johnson's mother during their official visit to Austin, she tried to close the deal for the Longhorns.

"My mom met Coach Brown on my visit," Johnson said. "I tell you what—the older I get the more I appreciate his recruiting style. He literally had my mom, after we left, like, 'Derrick, we need to sign up. I mean, you only have a certain amount of scholarships, you know.' This and that. 'You've got to get one.' I told her that I think they wanted me, so they'd wait a little bit. Let me take this recruiting process and take it all in and go visit here and there. I've always been a Texas leaner when it comes to that. They kind of knew that, but you never know what young kids will do when they go to different places and they get influenced by different teams and different colleges. The good thing I like about Mack, he didn't lie to me either. You know a lot of these coaches say, 'Man, you're gonna start,' because I was a big linebacker All-American and all that stuff. So they kind of tell these guys, 'You're gonna do this, you're gonna play, you're gonna be the staple.' That kind of gets the kids excited and gets them on board. Mack told me they had three senior linebackers. 'We'll try to play you this year, but after this year, it will be wide open.' Obviously, when I came in I performed better than they thought and I broke into that three-man rotation with Tyrone Jones, Everick Rawls, and D.D. Lewis. They've been starting for three years, and I was this young freshman kid. I was this skinny kid coming in and breaking it up, but they took me in. They were great, great mentors for me."

The Red River serves as the northern border of the state of Texas, separating it from Oklahoma. That river serves as the central battle line for high-profile recruitments year after year. While Oklahoma high school football has its share of good players, nothing compares to the wealth of talent in the state of Texas. The Sooners have made their living dipping into the Lone Star State every year and winning battles against programs such as TCU, Baylor, Texas, and Texas A&M. Johnson had dreams of staying in his home state, but the pull from Oklahoma dropped Texas A&M to a distant third on his list and provided the Longhorns with a strong challenge for one of the nation's best defenders.

"OU. I hate to say it, but it was OU," Johnson said. "There was a lot of Texas guys there, especially at that time. I knew all of the OU players and the guys that were trying to go to OU. Tommie Harris was a good friend of mine when we were coming out. He was a guy that—we will still go back and forth to this day—but I just knew he was going to Texas. He'll talk about [how] he thought I was going to OU, but Tommie knew I wasn't going there in the end. We had already talked about it. We went on our visit and all that together. He knew I was a Texas leaner, and once he found out through the grapevine—he went to OU and I committed to Texas—he was congratulatory, and everything was fine. OU was my second choice. They were on me hard and really aggressive. I think Texas A&M would have been second, but OU was really adamant about having me. I really liked that at that time, even though I was going to be in foreign territory. Thinking about going to Norman still gives me a headache to this day, even though they were great."

State pride can often be a big factor in recruiting, and coaches know they either have to play to that feeling or play against it if they are outside of that player's state. Brown went heavy on the pitch of staying in Texas and representing the Longhorns. Johnson always leaned toward Texas, and the Longhorns would eventually win despite not being one of the top programs in the country at the time.

"I did," Johnson said. "And that was Coach Brown's spiel too. He knew OU was in the mix and he knew Texas A&M was in the mix. He told me that if I want to stay in Texas and have my mom be able to ride down 1 hour and 15 minutes to the game, Texas is the spot. On top of that, I could get a great education, play on the biggest stage nationally, and play for a program that was getting better. Really, at that time, Texas was just okay. They were getting there, but they weren't doing what we were doing—winning 10 games every year like we did when I got there. They weren't on the low end, but at that time I just said I wanted to go to Texas and be a Longhorn. It's just something about being a Longhorn. I think me picking Texas had to do with not only everything they provide and Mack Brown and all of his recruiting tactics—I was personally a Texas leaner, so regardless, I was going to Texas at the end of the day."

That didn't stop some nationally ranked power players from trying to get into the race for Johnson. Florida State was the premier program in the country at the time, and Johnson had cousins who played for the Seminoles. Several other national title contenders also came calling, but Johnson wanted to stay home and close to his mother.

"I went to Florida State," Johnson said. "I'm a mama's boy. I was youngest in the family and the spoiled one, like my brothers and sisters say. I wasn't getting far away from home, but I had a cousin named Kevin Emanuel that played for Florida State, and they were on me. I went to a visit just to show good faith and go out of town. I didn't really like it, honestly. Penn State and Miami were always calling, but I kind of shut them down. I didn't want them to put all that effort in because I wasn't going. It wasn't even going to be possible for me to go. If I had gone out of state, it would have been OU or Florida State, but that would be a reach. My cousin was a couple of years older than me, and he would have been gone pretty quick. I was definitely staying close to home."

When it came time for Johnson to make his visits, Texas rolled out the red carpet. Rod Babers was his host player, but the trip was made up of one big group of players and recruits. That was spearheaded by Brown, who saw his football program as a giant family. That family environment was a huge weapon for Texas in recruiting, as players on the roster put aside their pride to help recruit younger players who were capable of taking their playing time. Brown served as a father figure to Johnson, who noted that he isn't surprised to see what Brown is doing in his second run as the head coach of North Carolina.

"Rod Babers was a great host," he said. "I remember—I think it was cold during that time. It was November or December, and I remember him having a black trench coat on. Rod did a great job. It wasn't just him, we all kind of went out together. They all kind of put their arms around us. It was a good time. Cedric Benson was on that trip, and there were a few guys who committed already, like Brian Carter and a lot of other guys. I think Mack Brown took pride in recruiting high-character guys. Not that we were perfect, but there were high-character guys who would bring us in where there wouldn't be any jealousy or pride. We're all trying to get better, and he built that from the ground up. He was definitely a second father figure for us. That's what he was to me. He was always gracious to me, and he loves my mom to this day. When I see Mack Brown the first thing he asks is how my mom is doing. He's still recruiting—I'm not surprised by how he's done at North Carolina. That's just what he does. He's a facilitator. He's not that coach that's like, 'You've got to make sure you run this slant right here and do this and do that.' He's not coaching like that. He's getting the right people in spots like he's the president. He's the big brains of the operation, and he gets the right coaches in spots and he knows how to do that. He's actually harder on the coaches than he is on the players. The players love him, and if you ask the coaches, it's a lot different for them."

Johnson made sure to take all of his visits. After seeing four of the top programs he was considering, Johnson decided to narrow his list down to rivals Texas and Oklahoma.

"I can't remember which one I took first," Johnson said. "Texas A&M was a pretty good visit, it just seemed like I was out in the boonies. I was just looking around and didn't know where I was, but they were really nice to me. After I took my visits to Texas, Texas A&M, OU, and Florida State, I was going to take Arkansas. My brother had a connection with Houston Nutt because he was all over my brother at the time of his recruitment. I was going to go visit, but I thought to myself, 'Why would I go to Arkansas? That's a waste of time for me.' I could go and eat their food and do all that stuff, but I just told them I wasn't coming. Right after that, I narrowed it down to OU and Texas. Even though I say it was out of those two, Texas was a lot higher in my mind than OU. I picked Texas, and that's the best decision I ever made."

Growing up a Baylor fan, Johnson said he gave the Bears plenty of consideration. While Baylor didn't make its way into his list of finalists, he did meet with the coaches a few times. Despite his older brother playing at the local university, his family made sure he knew there was no pressure to end up in the Green and Gold.

"If it was today, Baylor would be in the mix," Johnson said. "They'd be in the top three. Not that I would pick them over Texas, but they would be in the top five for sure. I'm a Waco kid, but I had seen too much. My brother even told me not to feel any pressure to go to Baylor because he went there. I really looked up to my brother. He was a big-time mentor for me, but he said I needed to make my own path. Underneath he was telling me to do me. He started there, but he lost a lot of games during that time. I don't know if he really wanted me to go through that. Baylor came to the house. I listened. I would never be rude; I'm not that guy. I shut it down pretty early though."

Official visits are usually full of parties, and Texas was no different at the time. Johnson was a sheltered kid who didn't indulge in that life until he got into college, but it was everywhere around him. Johnson said that aside from the family aspect of Texas, there weren't a ton of memorable stories, but they did end up having a strong class.

"I don't have many stories," Johnson said. "I became a party guy and did my college stuff maybe after my sophomore year where I got out there and enjoyed it—maybe a little bit too much. At that time I was a small-town kid that went to church every weekend and church during the week. My mom was big with the youth in the community and a schoolteacher, so I was kind of grounded. I wasn't a perfect kid, but if I saw something, I usually stayed out of it. I'm glad I didn't jump into that because I was inexperienced at that whole life. I wouldn't have known how to manage it. I don't have many crazy stories, I just remember that me and Cedric Benson were always the two big-time guys on these visits. We had a great class when you talk about Michael Huff, Michael Griffin, Jonathan Scott—we all did well. Aaron Ross was in the class, but he had to prolong his signing two years because of academics, but we had a good class."

Johnson and Cedric Benson both were cornerstones of the class and would provide a strong foundation for the future. Benson was a mythical figure in Texas high school circles. The Midland Lee (now called Midland Legacy) running back led the Rebels to three consecutive state titles, rushing for 8,423 yards over his career at the 5A level, which served as the highest classification in the state at the time. The two became close during their recruitment and early time on campus.

"If you didn't know who Cedric Benson was, you were living under a rock in Texas," Johnson said. "We'd see him on TV all the time as a kid. It was No. 32 getting the ball over 40 times in high school. You couldn't stop him. He had some crazy numbers, and he was my freshman roommate. You talk about someone I'm close to and someone I knew—we knew each other really well. It's pretty cool because I got my respect from Cedric out there on the field. Cedric had the ultimate confidence. He thought he could run through a wall, which helps him actually. When I got there, we were going against each other, and I was hitting him. He kind of knew me, but he didn't really know me like that. He was the top dog in the class, but he thought I was good. We used to practice just as freshmen, so coaches told him when they get with the other guys it won't be like that. I kind of got my respect real early, like I was one of the big dogs too."

Benson tragically passed away as the result of an automotive accident in August 2019. He was one of the more unique characters to ever come through Austin, and Johnson said that the only word he can think of to describe him is "different."

"That's the word you use with Cedric," Johnson said. "The other guys weren't crazy close with him, but they knew Ced, and they were cool with Ced. Everybody wasn't cool with Ced, because Ced has a personality that's a little different. He'd talk a lot, or he could be silent where you'd think he didn't like you. I was always at the top of that food chain. We were always really close. The one thing I remember about Ced is when we got there, we'd have to introduce ourselves in front of the upperclassmen. We were all nervous as freshmen. You had to say your name, your position, and your hometown. It was kind of nerve-racking for everyone. Cedric gets up there and says, 'I'm Cedric Benson from Midland Lee. Starting running back.' In front of everybody he did that. Everyone just kind of looked around, but I tell you what—he did start that year."

When the time came, Johnson made the phone call to his recruiter, Darryl Drake, to let him know he'd be headed to Austin. After calling Drake, Texas defensive coordinator Carl "Bull" Reese and Mack Brown called him to celebrate. Even with Johnson committed, the staff didn't make any promises they couldn't live up to. That was a huge reason why Johnson picked Texas in the first place.

"It was a phone call," Johnson said. "It was my senior year, and I called him up and told him I was coming. I told Coach Drake first, and he was so happy. Then Coach Reese and Coach Brown called me. They were so happy that I was going to be a Longhorn. They didn't promise me anything, and that's what I loved about it. Sometimes people promise things because that's what you do. They need to work their tail off and let the chips fall where they may."

Now that he was officially part of the Longhorn family, Johnson was one of the many young men unofficially adopted by team matriarch Sally Brown. Sally Brown served as a motherly figure to the young men in burnt orange, and she helped many who moved away from their own mothers feel comfortable in school. She and Coach Brown also helped show the players what a healthy and loving relationship looked like.

"Most of the players interact with their mom," Johnson said. "Especially African American players. We had a lot of players that were really close with their mom depending on what happened to their dad. Everyone can relate to a mom, and Sally was that second mom. She was very loving. She'd always give you a hug. She was always smiling. I never saw a bad moment with her. Marriages aren't always perfect, but that was a perfect situation for us to see that. Mack Brown never hid the fact that he loved his wife and loved her being around. Miss Sally was always around giving us cookies and all that stuff on game day. It was pretty cool now that you look back. At the time you don't really appreciate it, but you need that example of a man and a woman together like that in a healthy relationship.

"Sometimes my mindset was, by default, that I needed to think a little bit bigger because I had the goods and had the work ethic," Johnson said. "I needed to think a little bit bigger because going out there I knew I wasn't going to play. I might have to redshirt or just get in on special teams. I didn't want to redshirt because nobody does, and I was out there and going and making these plays. People were looking at me like I was going to play this year. I just thought because they had three senior linebackers, I wouldn't make a dent. My own classmates were telling me I was better than what was on the field. I was good with no distractions and just going to work."

Johnson played early and became a vital part of the Texas defense. Despite starting just two games that season, Johnson was second on the team in tackles. One of his two starts was the annual Red River Shootout against Oklahoma at the Cotton Bowl in Dallas. Johnson tallied eight tackles on that day to lead the Texas defense in a game that would ultimately be defined by Oklahoma's Roy Williams making a heroic play, flying over the top of the line and stripping the ball from Chris Simms for a Sooners touchdown.

"I had the most tackles that year on the team, but I only started two games," Johnson said. "What they did was, we beat a lot of people, so they'd get me in the game a lot in the second half. The OU game came up, or maybe it was Texas Tech. I know I started against Texas Tech and OU because they had the spread look. We were a 4-3 team, so we only had three linebackers. They were good at that time, but we had to go to a 3-4 just to stick me in there as an inside linebacker, and I played against OU. I started that freshman year. It was big for me to play in that game as a freshman. I did pretty well, but I only started two games and they stuck me in and out every other series, and I was able to get the most tackles on the team. When I got out there, I was doing what I needed to do."

There are many great rivalry games in college sports, but the annual matchup between Texas and Oklahoma—or Oklahoma and Texas, depending on what side of the rivalry you're on—stands out because of its unique backdrop and setup. Played at the State Fair of Texas in South Dallas on the second Saturday of every October, the game is one of major momentum swings as the two teams battle for bragging rights and the Golden Hat Trophy. Johnson said the game is singular in his mind when it comes to the environment.

"It was very special," Johnson said. "I looked forward to it every year regardless of us losing the big one. We got blown out one time and it was terrible. I loved that game. You talk about the atmosphere of the fairgrounds, where it's just packed. You're going in and fans are flipping you off. Then you see Texas fans, and you feel a little safer. If you can handle the emotion in that game, you can do well in it. I've had good numbers every year in that game. OU was really good during the time I was there—they went to two national championships. They were really good. You can name the Jason Whites, Tommie Harris Jr., Rocky Calmus, Brandon Everage, Derrick Strait, and all those guys. I knew all of them because they were all Texas guys. Mack Brown would tell the upperclassmen to get with us about the game so we wouldn't be surprised. You'd get the stories here and there about people flipping you off and it was going to be crazy, but you go, and it was like more than what you were told. It was one of those things that you have to experience to get the full view and perspective. It's an awesome game. It still gives me chills to this day thinking about that game. I've been in some big games in college and in the NFL during my 14 years, and that game still sticks out."

Johnson went on to finish his freshman year with 83 tackles, 13 tackles for loss, and 4.5 sacks. His performance earned him freshman All-America honors, and he was named the Big 12 Co-Defensive Freshman of the Year. He was named the Defensive MVP of the Holiday Bowl against No. 21 Washington after recording nine tackles, a sack, and an interception that led to UT's first go-ahead TD in the fourth quarter. Johnson officially took his place as a stalwart within the defense during that game as well, replacing senior linebacker Everick Rawls on a full-time basis after rotating back and forth.

"I didn't even start that game either," Johnson said. "Sitting here thinking about it, I was thinking maybe if I started, I'd have way more stats. It actually helped to keep me on my toes and to have a sense of urgency to make a play. I knew I was only getting about half of the game. As I was doing good throughout the year, they started switching us more. It was the first time they kind of benched Everick Rawls. We were going back and forth, but I started playing really good. I got a big sack, and then they let me play like the last few series of the game. I'm a team guy, and I looked at Everick like it sucks, but at the same time I knew the situation. I got an interception after that. It was rolling and everybody was hyped, so that was a pretty cool moment for me."

Johnson would move forward as a leader on the team, working to help the program reach the next level. It was during his sophomore year that he crossed paths with a lanky freshman named Vince Young. Young would go on to lead Texas to a national title in 2005, but he had to develop as a passer when he first got to college. Johnson and the rest of the team could feel Young had something special in store, and Johnson knew after playing in his final game that his team would likely go on to win a championship the next year without him.

"We knew he was this crazy athlete, but we knew you had to throw the ball," Johnson said. "We didn't know when he was going to be able to throw it. We knew he was pretty confident in throwing the ball and that he could run, but once he put it all together, we knew something would happen because he's the guy. You could see it my last year, especially with the Michigan game and everything. The next year it really turned on that he had arrived, and nobody could handle him. I was pretty sure leaving in '05 that they would win it all. It was just me and Cedric that left, so all the people that came in with me were still playing. I knew they had a great team and a veteran team. With the way Vince was growing coming off of the Michigan game, we already knew they would be. It's bittersweet because I put in so much work during that time, and I just missed it by a year. Honestly I've gotten used to that. I retired in 2018 and the Chiefs won in '19. You talk about just missing it by a year—that's my life story."

As a sophomore, Johnson registered 120 tackles and four interceptions as the Longhorns went 11–2 and beat LSU in the Cotton Bowl on New Year's Day. Texas was primed to take the next step but fell to 10–3 in 2003 with losses to Arkansas and Oklahoma and an embarrassing performance against Washington State in the Holiday Bowl. As Johnson entered his senior season, he developed a new weapon to add to his arsenal: when trailing ball carriers from behind, Johnson would secure the tackle with one arm and punch from behind to knock the ball out. It was such an effective move that Johnson would go on to force nine fumbles in 2004, tying him atop the all-time NCAA list for a single season at the time. To put into perspective how big his performance was that year, Johnson forced a fumble on 1 out of every 14 tackles he made.

"I was working on it in practice going into my senior year," Johnson said. "It was coming out, and I was thinking it was pretty easy. I was tracking these guys down, securing the tackle, and then knocking it out from the back. I decided to be intentional about it in the games and try it. I did it the first game against North Texas and knocked it out. I just started being intentional about working on it in practice, and coaches saw that. We just kept working on it, and when I was in the game I would run them down on a toss play, and, instead of hitting them from the side, I'd wrap that arm to secure the tackle and wrap my other arm around to knock the ball out. It happened a lot."

Texas had national title aspirations in 2004, but once again Oklahoma stood in the way. The Longhorns lost 12–0 to Oklahoma in Dallas that year, capping Johnson's college career with a 0–4 record against the Sooners. Going into the season, the national title was the ultimate goal. Texas players knew they had the pieces in place to make a run.

"That was the goal," Johnson said. "Looking back, we thought Vince was ready. We didn't know he had even more to him, and we saw that the next year. During 2004 we thought we were ready because we had a lot of upperclassmen, and Vince was in his third year as a redshirt sophomore. He was doing well, and we just capped it off at that because we had all the pieces. Cedric was eating it up with Vince in the backfield running the zone read—people couldn't stop it."

If Texas wanted a shot at that title, they would need to win out and hope for an Oklahoma loss. Disaster almost struck a few weeks later when Oklahoma State took a 35–14 lead into the half, but a ferocious second-half effort from Texas allowed the Longhorns to come roaring back to win. Johnson was huge in the effort, with 18 tackles. That game ignited the rest of the Texas season and pushed them into position to win it all in 2005.

"It was 35–7, and I think we scored right before the half," Johnson said. "They had a 21-point lead, and they were doing whatever they wanted to us. We went into the locker room thinking we couldn't lose again because we'd already lost to OU, and we wanted to get to the national championship. Mack Brown wasn't cussing and fussing in there. He told us we were going to go out and they weren't going to score again. He told us to go show the world who we were. The ending score was 56–35. It was crazy."

Johnson was able to take part in a special tradition at The University of Texas during his senior year. During his final home game at Darrell K Royal-Texas Memorial Stadium, Johnson donned No. 60 to honor legendary Texas linebacker Tommy Nobis Jr. Nobis was a star at Texas, helping the Longhorns win the national championship in 1963 before being selected first overall by the Atlanta Falcons in the 1966 NFL Draft.

"It was a tradition for really great linebackers at Texas," Johnson said. "If you were the guy, you got to pay homage to Tommy. Some guys wore the number as their regular number, but I was a little too new-school to wear 60. I wanted to do it during my last game at DKR. I had a pretty good game. I don't take that for granted at all. My second or third year they wanted me to put that on because I was the guy, but I wanted to make 11 great too. I always paid homage to Tommy Nobis, and I talked to him a few times during my time there, but it was pretty cool to end off my senior year at DKR with that number on."

His final college game was played at the historic Rose Bowl on New Year's Day against Michigan. In a game that ended on a Texas field goal as time expired, the Longhorns won 38–37. Vince Young dominated the day, and Johnson had the most lackluster performance of his career, notching only two tackles and a forced fumble. Still it was an incredible game to be a part of, and he was happy to go out with a win. Johnson was named an All-American and earned the Bronko Nagurski Trophy as the nation's top defensive player and the Butkus Award as the nation's top linebacker.

"Michigan was a really good team," Johnson said. "They obviously could have won that game as well, with Braylon Edwards and all of those guys on there. That's the only big game that I look back and think I didn't perform like I wanted to. Even though we won, we won because of Vince. We won because of his play. He may have better numbers that game than he did during the national championship game. He was on. It was a very exciting game. It was good to cap my senior year off with a win. If I had a fifth year, I would have stayed at Texas. Even my junior year, people were saying I could come out and be a late first rounder or a second-round pick, but I didn't want to come out. I had one more year at Texas and was with all of my guys. I was in no rush to get into that life. It was pretty cool to win my last one at Texas and cap off the year winning the Nagurski and Butkus Award[s]."

Johnson was selected in the first round of the 2005 NFL Draft by the Kansas City Chiefs. During a 14-year career spent mainly in

Kansas City with a short stop in Oakland, Johnson was a four-time Pro Bowl selection and two-time All-Pro. He retired in 2018 as the all-time leading tackler in Kansas City's history. Now back in Austin, Johnson tries to spend time around the program whenever possible, although the COVID-19 pandemic in 2020 made dropping by more challenging, and Johnson is also typically engaged with his wife and six children.

"I live in Austin, so every other game I'm there," Johnson said. "If there are six games there, I'm at least there for four of them. I'm always in someone's suite or on the sideline or something. I want to be there even more, but I have six kiddos, so I can't be around like I want to. I think also COVID has put a little bit of distance between us as well. You just can't show up, and you probably wouldn't want to at this time anyway. I've talked to Coach Sarkisian a few times and had a few conversations with him. He's a guy that's easy to talk to. Some head coaches can make you feel uptight, but Sark is a very cool guy. He's really relaxed and a player's coach. He knows his stuff and he's put together a good coaching staff. He just needs to get some more wins."

Johnson finished his college degree after retiring from the NFL and graduated from Texas in 2019. Nowadays he spends his time relaxing and providing analysis on football through social media. He's also heavily involved in giving back through his Defend the Dream Foundation that helps provide library books to schools in low-income areas.

"I don't have the time right now, so I'm just coaching from the couch," Johnson said. "I'm always doing little radio shows or analysis for the Chiefs and putting it out on Twitter. I'm a philanthropist. I'm big with my foundation, which caters to inner-city kids through education. It's called Defend the Dream, and I love that. It's strictly about getting age-appropriate new books and making over their libraries at Title I schools. These are schools that need help with their libraries to liven it up and bring a whole bunch of new books in at a low-income area to help get their reading level up. I'm not doing much other than that."

Johnson always described himself as a "Texas leaner." Looking back over his recruitment and career, everything played out the way he wanted it to. Asked if he'd do anything differently, Johnson only said he would have been better about networking and using his status as a football player to help serve him down the line.

"I wouldn't do anything different," Johnson said. "Not at all. I'd still take my visits because I think it's good to see other things, but I always go with my gut feeling. My gut feeling was that I was a Texas guy, and I was going to be a Longhorn. I couldn't wait to play in Austin. I do think I would be more intentional while I was at Texas about networking and meeting people. I do that now, but during that time you're so focused on football you don't shake enough hands and keep enough numbers or business cards."

CHAPTER 2

Blake Brockermeyer

If you spend any amount of time around Blake Brockermeyer, you'd think he was always meant to be a Texas Longhorn. He may have grown up the son of former Texas offensive lineman Kay Brockermeyer, but he never intended that for himself. While Texas was struggling through the late '80s, Brockermeyer had his sights set on other destinations.

"I don't know why, but UCLA was always the school I always watched as a kid," Brockermeyer said. "They were always a good team. I remember watching them and Michigan and all these different schools. You know, my dad—my mom and dad had gone to Texas, but besides A&M, which I never liked, the Texas teams weren't that good. The Southwest Conference didn't do a whole lot for me. You know, TCU wasn't very good, and I didn't want to stay at home anyway. Texas had not been very good the last few years, and so really I thought if I wanted to get to play somewhere, at first you don't really know who's going to recruit you. Then after a while I was like, 'Qow, like, I've got all these crazy schools recruiting me that I didn't expect.' So I really just wanted to go out of state. I had no desire to play anywhere in Texas—like I was 100 percent going out of state for the longest time. When I did my official visits I didn't have an official visit in the state of Texas at first. I mean, I had to drop a school to take the Texas visit."

Brockermeyer was a standout at Arlington Heights High School in Fort Worth. Though his dad had his own glory on the field, Kay never pushed Blake to attend Texas. In fact Blake was never even immersed in the UT culture growing up.

"Even though my dad played there, it wasn't something that was talked about a lot. He was very much about going to college to get an education," Brockermeyer said. "He grew up in Fort Worth and was from very humble beginnings. He played football and went to college and got to law school. His education was his path to his future where, you know, most kids now it's like football is their major. At my house that was not the case. And my brother had gone to USC. And so we never went to games—we didn't have season tickets. It was just kind of like it wasn't a big deal. I think I went to a Texas-TCU game at TCU in like '88 or something. I think I remember going to a Texas game in Fort Worth, but I didn't watch them on TV. I was hunting and fishing, and I wouldn't sit around and just watch football all day long."

Brockermeyer knew he would be recruited early in his high school career, but a strong performance against another top prospect put him on the radar for real.

"My freshman year, I was probably 6'0", 170," Brockermeyer said. "I had a good frame on me, and we had a pretty good team that year. Going into my sophomore year, I actually was coming off like a dislocated kneecap deal that I had. I'd gotten big—I was like 205—and they wanted me to play varsity. But I remember I had to, like, pass all these little tests with my knee. I missed half the season, I think, my sophomore year—if I remember correctly—but then toward the end of my sophomore year, I started feeling better and kind of got out on the field. But then my junior year I had what was probably my big breakthrough year. I played against a guy from Trimble Tech named Henry Ford, who went to Arkansas. And he was [a] senior—he was a highly recruited guy. He had all these offers and whatever, and I had a good game against him. Once that game ended, I started getting a bunch of stuff from schools."

Once he had a few options at his disposal, Brockermeyer and his father started to weed through the schools recruiting him. A trip to South Bend to see one of college football's most hallowed campuses didn't turn out the way he thought it would.

"After my junior year, I took a bunch of unofficial visits," Brockermeyer said. "I went to Notre Dame for their spring game. Lou Holtz was there, and I hated it. My dad and I couldn't figure out why anyone would want to go there. My trainers in town—one of them was an Aggie—they made me go to a TCU-A&M game. I knew I wasn't going to go to A&M, but I did it just because of him. Notre Dame, I remember, was a big deal. They had just won the national championship. I thought it was going to be this amazing place, but it turned out to be the opposite."

Brockermeyer would later watch three of his sons go through the modern recruiting process full of offers, social media, crazed fans, and more. For him in the early '90s, the process was much less formal.

"There weren't these official offers and stuff that they do now, and there was no Internet," Brockermeyer said. "There was lots of mail. In fact I have most of it. You used to have to get on the phone with them so they could call you anytime, as much as they wanted. There were no dead periods—as far as I know, there weren't."

Florida State was a national power when Brockermeyer was entering his recruitment. The Seminoles targeted and recruited him harder than anyone.

"Florida State was the best team in the country back then, and they recruited me relentlessly, like crazy," Brockermeyer said. "I mean, I was like the No. 1 player in the country for them. So I'd gone to the Florida State–Florida game. It was the same day that A&M and Texas were playing, I think. It was in Tallahassee, and I remember going to the game. It was the big game that was a huge deal—and Florida State, you know, they were one of the top-five teams in the country for like a decade. I was just like, 'I can't believe these guys want me this bad.' I played at a terrible school. We might have won 10 games in my three years of playing varsity there. I mean we were horrible. I never understood why they wanted me so bad."

Brockermeyer was ready to be a Seminole, but his parents stood in the way. Despite not being hands-on with his recruitment, they were adamant that they didn't want him at Florida State. That decision alone put the Longhorns back into the picture.

"Of all the schools, that's where I was going to go for a long time," Brockermeyer said. "My parents were like, 'You're not going there.' They said I could go anywhere else. 'But you're not going to Florida State.' I think it was just they felt like it was just a bad school. But after that visit I was going to take my last official visit there, and I was going to commit. Back then you took all your officials after the season, and you had basically five weekends to go. And so you take your five trips, and you're done. When that went out of the picture, that's where Texas kind of got back in the picture."

With Florida State eliminated, Brockermeyer next looked to the Pacific Northwest as a likely destination.

"Washington was a huge player," Brockermeyer said. "They were my second choice. I knew Florida State and Washington would win a national championship—it was just a lock. And sure enough Washington won one my freshman year and Florida State won my sophomore year. I mean, I knew they would win it—there's no way they wouldn't. Washington should have won it the year before, but they blew it against UCLA."

While Brockermeyer decided between Texas and Washington, he took official trips to UCLA, Colorado, and Tennessee for fun. Though Brockermeyer grew up wanting to play for the Bruins, he knew where he was headed by the time he visited.

"I'd gone to Texas the week before, and I knew I was going there at that point," Brockermeyer said. "So I had one more trip to go, and I was thinking I should go to Arizona State or UCLA and have some fun. Tennessee and Colorado were the other two teams I took officials to, and Colorado was hot at the time—they had a couple of linemen get drafted. Tennessee had two first-round picks get drafted on the offensive line."

Brockermeyer first heard from Texas before his senior year. He was contacted by his area recruiter and offensive line coach Clovis Hale. As he went into his official visits, Brockermeyer wanted to take the process with enough seriousness to make a decision, but he also wanted to have fun with it. Seeing different parts of the world made Texas feel all the more familiar in the long run.

"I looked at it as like a huge party," Brockermeyer said. "I was going to go out and have fun—party—but at the same time, I've got to make a decision. I knew how serious it was because there's no transfer portal. Back then it was like when you go somewhere, your ass was stuck there. So as I started taking my visits—I went to Tennessee, I went to Colorado, I went to Washington—the people out of the state of Texas are different than Texans. That's what I noticed. And so, even though I liked some of these places and I thought, you know, this is going to be a good team. The people were different."

It didn't hurt the Longhorns that they appeared to be trending up in the college football world. In 1990 Texas won the Southwest Conference and finished in the top 15 in the country. Despite a blowout loss to Miami in the Cotton Bowl, the Longhorns appeared to be headed for great success.

"Texas had a really good year that year, which, if they hadn't had that, there's no way I would have gone there," Brockermeyer said. "They'd gone to the Cotton Bowl, and Miami beat them by 100. That was kind of the end of the year. I'd gone to the Texas-OU game that year, where one of the Cash brothers scored a touchdown to win it toward the end of the game. I went on Oklahoma's tickets because Oklahoma was a home team, so I had to go, like, on their ticket, but I was rooting for Texas. There's no way in hell I was going to OU. I had seen them a little bit. I was like, 'Hey, you know, these guys are on the—they're on the come-up a little bit.' I'm not going to Colorado for sure and definitely not going to Tennessee. Washington I loved, and I really wanted to go to Washington, but I didn't want to make my family fly to Seattle every week or wherever you're playing. So it got down at the end to be Texas and Washington."

While Brockermeyer was choosing to stay at home or head to Seattle, his parents were working behind the scenes. Although they hadn't interfered much in his recruitment to that point, they went behind his back for a meeting with the Texas coaches.

"My parents had gone down to Austin the week before I had gone on my visit," Brockermeyer said. "Basically I found out later they told them like, 'Whatever you got to do, get him to go here. We want him here.' They never told me that, but I found that out later. Scott Gooch told me he hadn't, probably, cleaned his room up in a year—it just so happened that day or day before that my parents came to the dorm, they knocked on the door and, like, their room was clean. But they basically told Scott like, 'Whatever you have to do to get him to go to Texas, get him to go there.'"

Once the official visit came, Texas was able to solidify its position with a strong trip. Brockermeyer was hosted by former Longhorn Scott Gooch, who remains a friend to this day, and he certainly enjoyed himself on his trip.

"It was fun," Brockermeyer said. "I remember back then you [could] take a private jet. So we took a private jet with a couple other guys. There's like three or four or five of us in this little plane. And so we had a booster's plane that took us down to Austin, which I thought was pretty cool. Scott Gooch was my recruiting host, who I'd never heard of. On my Washington visit, Steve Emtman was my recruiting host. He won the Outland and Lombardi Trophies. He was Mr. Badass. They made me a big priority. I just remember we partied a lot. I remember that for sure. We went out. One night we ate in the press box, and one night we went down to—I think it was Lake Austin—to a place they used to take everybody back then. I just remember we had a lot of fun."

Brockermeyer didn't have much guidance or an idea as far as what to look for in each school. He was able to scrape together a checklist on his own, but it wasn't as detailed as he would have liked it to be.

"The media guide was a big deal back then," he said. "The NCAA basically banned it at some point because teams are doing media guides that were, you know, back at the time, 200 pages. The bigger and flashier the media guide—it was a recruiting deal. I'd gone through the rosters and to see where I could play early. And so I looked at that and the strength coach. I had kind of learned along the way that was going to be someone that you were going to spend a lot of time with. I wanted to get to know the strength coaches and who they were and kind of see if I vibe with those guys or not. So I knew a little bit, but from what my kids know and what I knew is a big difference."

One reason the Longhorns were able to cement themselves with him was a connection with the Texas strength and conditioning staff.

"I really connected with Dana LeDuc, the strength coach. Oskar Jacobson was the assistant strength coach. So I felt kind of good about that when I was there, and just the guys on the team, I felt like I got along with and kind of connected with them. They were Texans. I mean, back then, like, everyone [at] Texas was a Texan for the most part. They might have had one or two guys that weren't. I remember going into Coach McWilliams' office on Sunday where he had the exit interview where you talk about the trip. I knew when I left there—like I didn't make a commitment then, but I think I committed shortly after. But I remember leaving there saying, 'Yeah, I'm gonna go to Texas.'"

His parents' wishes had paid off. After working behind the scenes to make sure his visit would keep him close to home, he was leaning toward Texas. His parents were excited about the possibilities.

"I think they were excited," Brockermeyer said. "It worked out great because they went to all my games. They went to all their away games, home games—like they went to everything. I have no [doubt] I would—if I had to do [it] over again—I'd do the exact same thing I did. I wish we could have won more, but I think if I had the knowledge that I have now, it might have been [a] different deal, but I didn't know. I didn't have a lot of great guidance. My parents were like, 'Go wherever you want to go.' I really wanted to get to Washington, but I just didn't want to put everyone through that. It turned out good, because Washington was really good, but then after that they got on probation."

Brockermeyer met his future wife, Kristy, during high school, and the two attended Texas together. Even though they were sweethearts at Arlington Heights, Brockermeyer wasn't going to let anyone else dictate his decision. Despite that, it still worked out for the best.

"So we graduated from high school, and she literally left the next day to go down to enroll in summer school. She had to make a certain GPA to get in. I thought it was crazy. If you went exactly however many hours that they made you go, they guaranteed you that you'd get into Texas. So she did that and got in. I think TCU [was] her second option. But she was always dead set on going to Texas unless for some weird reason she didn't get in. Whatever grade she needed to make she made. I think it was like a 3.0. It definitely helped, but it wasn't like wherever she goes, I'm going to school. I think the Texas thing started to check a lot of boxes off."

Brockermeyer eventually gave his commitment to Texas head coach David McWilliams. A former Longhorn himself, McWilliams played on the 1963 team that won the first national championship in the career of legendary head coach Darrell K Royal. McWilliams returned to Austin as an assistant under Royal in the '70s and served as the defensive coordinator for his alma mater under Fred Akers in the '80s. After taking the head coaching job at Texas Tech, McWilliams came back home to Austin to resurrect the program. While he looked like the right man to get the job done, his tenure would come to an end just one year later.

"He was a super nice guy," Brockermeyer said. "I mean, the Texas deal to me—I felt like their program was on the come-up. So I thought these other programs I knew were going to win big, but Texas was kind of, I guess you could say, it's kind of like they are now—but it didn't turn out that way. It turned out where basically [of] all the schools I could have gone to, Texas actually was probably the worst school on the field, which was kind of disappointing looking back on it. I'm still friends with him. When I made the Hall of Honor, he called me. His son's at SMU, so I would see him once or twice a year at SMU. You know, just a good guy."

Once McWilliams resigned, Texas turned next to a proven winner in John Mackovic. After serving as the head coach for the Kansas City Chiefs in the NFL and the University of Illinois, Mackovic was looked upon as the next in line to revive the Texas program. For Brockermeyer this was a blessing, considering he didn't see eye to eye with McWilliams' offensive line coach, Clovis Hale.

"I didn't vibe with him very much," Brockermeyer said. "And fortunately—or unfortunately—they all got let go after my first year. The coach that came in after that, Pat Watson, we got along great. He passed away like 15 years ago, probably. I think he played at Mississippi State. He had been on the Georgia Tech national championship team that tied Colorado. He had coached Georgia. I think he coached at Clemson, and that was a big upgrade for me. I connected with him. I just remember my first year there I redshirted. I was a really good run blocker, but we didn't throw the ball in high school. I had no idea, and no one had taught me anything. I just remember sitting back and just watching the older guys and trying to, you know, figure it all out. And then in the spring of my freshman year, like something just clicked."

Growing up in Fort Worth, Brockermeyer had been to the Texas State Fairgrounds before to see the Cotton Bowl. Despite seeing some of the best in college football play in the New Year's Day bowl game, nothing matched the intensity of the annual matchup that took place on the second Saturday in October between Texas and Oklahoma.

"I can't remember how, but my dad had had a friend or someone he knew that had Cotton Bowl tickets every year," Brockermeyer said. "And so I had gone to the Cotton Bowl before and watched, I think, Arkansas. I can't remember who they played, but I remember UCLA and Arkansas. Troy Aikman was in the Cotton Bowl, so whoever that was around those years. For some reason, Tennessee, I think, was in it one year. So I'd been to the Cotton Bowl, but it wasn't like that game. And I remember thinking, 'Wow, this is pretty cool.' To this day I love that game.

"It was ridiculous. My redshirt freshman year I remember starting and playing. I was going against a guy who was supposed to be this ridiculous player. I was like, 'I can't believe I'm playing this game.' In your freshman year you're kind of thrown out to the wolves and thrown into the fire. You think you're doing a good job, but, looking back on it now, you probably weren't doing very good. But my sophomore year I was starting to be pretty good. That's like the third, fourth, fifth game of the year usually. You kind of start thinking sometimes you're better than you probably are. And I remember going out there and then, like the first play of the game, hitting someone. There was blood splattered all over my face mask, and I was like, 'Oh, yeah, I remember this.' Then my last year—my junior year—I was going against a good player. That was a big game. It was the Stonie Clark game. I knew going into my junior year that was going to probably be my last year. You look at things a lot differently. You kind of soak it in. You want to win that game your last year."

After redshirting his first year, Brockermeyer left Austin after his junior season in 1994 to pursue a job in professional football. His father met with several agents including Tom Condon, Leigh Steinberg, and Marvin Demoff, whom he eventually signed with. At that time, training for the NFL Combine wasn't what it is today. Brockermeyer stayed in school and finished his degree during his final spring semester, but that might not have happened had he known what he knows today.

"IMG were like the first people that I talked to that I'd ever heard of say, 'You can come train with us and do this.' I was thinking, 'Why would I want to do that? I'm just going to train in Austin with my strength coaches I've been working with.' If I had a crystal ball and could see the future, that was the future. I took a bunch of hours. I think I ended up taking like 18 or 19 hours. I ended up doing a lot of school my last semester. I trained hard, but I didn't really know what I was doing. And, you know, it worked out, but I feel like had I known then what I know now—like everybody now has it to [a] science—I would have definitely dropped out of school. But they weren't doing that back then. I ran my 40 in tennis shoes. I had a lot of bad advice. I feel like I could have helped myself more in that last semester training for all that. Even though I got drafted, I probably could have gotten drafted so much higher if I had known what the hell I was doing."

Brockermeyer was selected by the Carolina Panthers in the first round with the 29th overall pick in the 1995 NFL Draft. He and Kristy were married in 1996. Together they had four sons: Jack, Luke, and twins Tommy and James. While his father didn't act as a fan of his alma mater while Brockermeyer was growing up, that changed once he was officially on the roster. His parents had always supported him, but Kay Brockermeyer went above and beyond. And once Blake's sons were old enough to be recruited, Kay was even more interested in the process.

"Once I went there, he was all in, and, still to this day, he keeps up with what's going on. It's funny—this whole thing with my kids just basically did a complete circle. I mean it was like me again with my kids. It's almost like déjà vu."

Luke Brockermeyer followed in his father's footsteps, though he took a more unconventional route. After graduating from All Saints' Episcopal School in Fort Worth, Luke was prepared to accept a scholarship to Rice University over offers from Air Force Academy and Oregon State. Ranked a three-star player by the industry-generated 247Sports Composite Rankings, Luke was looking at the possibility of playing two sports at the collegiate level. When Texas head coach Tom Herman offered Luke a preferred walk-on spot, he jumped all over it and bet on himself. Though Brockermeyer didn't necessarily agree with the decision to walk on, it ended up working out. Luke was awarded a scholarship in 2020 and started in 2021 as an inside linebacker under first-year head coach Steve Sarkisian.

"I always tell my kids, 'Put it on film and the eye in the sky won't lie,'" Brockermeyer said. "Luke put it on film, and there was nothing. I was just like, 'Man, I don't know what else you have to do.' It was really disappointing that he didn't get anything. I knew he was a good player. He was a little bit undersized, but he was also going to play baseball in college. So we just said, you know, 'Hey, great junior year,' and we told him to go for it. It just didn't work out the way I had—or he had—thought it was going to happen. But, you know, Luke was really determined. He was open to go a lot of different places, but the other places weren't going for him. I wasn't real wild about him going to Texas because I just felt like they didn't really want him. Anyone will take a walk-on, right? I just felt like he would get lost in the shuffle and wouldn't be appreciated very much, but he didn't care. He wanted to go to Texas, and he said, 'You know, if I'm going to play, I'm going to have to beat out all these great people. Texas' linebacker situation is not the greatest situation on earth either. I think I have a chance down the road.' It's funny that [Todd] Orlando hit the nail right on the top of the head, man. He said, 'You know, Luke's a developmental player. You know, in three years I think he'll be ready to play.' And sure enough it's year three for him, and he finally got to play."

When it came time for his youngest sons to be recruited, the game had changed completely. Tommy Brockermeyer earned five-star status on every major recruiting site and he earned All-America honors in high school. James bloomed a bit later, but he eventually earned four-star status and 17 collegiate offers. Both players would have been welcomed additions at Texas, but the Longhorns were sinking under Tom Herman while Alabama was cementing its status as the greatest dynasty in collegiate history under legendary coach Nick Saban. It took going against convention and the wishes of some members of the family, but the twins chose to play for the Crimson Tide. It didn't help that Herman had offered James a walk-on spot just before Iowa reached out and offered him a full scholarship.

"My dad was not happy my other kids didn't go to Texas," Brockermeyer said. "I mean, I wanted them to go to Texas too. They made the decision at the end of the day, so it's not my decision to make. All I could do is educate them on, you know, things to look for and think about. When James got offered by Alabama it was really over at that point. Tommy really wanted to go to school with James."

Brockermeyer's parents were adamant that they didn't want him to attend Florida State. When it came time for James and Tommy to be recruited, Brockermeyer had only one hard-and-fast rule.

"With A&M I did for sure," Brockermeyer said. "I was even open—well, I wasn't open— but Oklahoma has such an incredible offense you at least have to think about it. I knew they wouldn't. My kids are Longhorn born and bred their whole life, so there was no way they'd go to Oklahoma."

Brockermeyer left Texas after starting all 34 games he played in, earning All-SWC honors two years in a row and All-America honors in 1994. He played in the NFL for eight years for the Panthers, Bears, and Broncos. After he returned home, he coached his kids in youth sports before getting into the college ranks and serving as an assistant at SMU under Sonny Dykes. With his recruitment and career behind him, his only regret is that he didn't do more in college.

"My only regret in college was that we didn't win more," Brockermeyer said. "For my kids, that's a big deal. If you're going to go do all this bullshit—I mean, they kill you in college—so you might as well win, right? I feel like I had it easy in college. I don't remember hardly ever getting up in the morning and working out. We worked out at 3:00 in the afternoon every day. I felt like it's a whole different thing. My only regret is that I wish I could have done things better. That probably would have helped our team out better if I was a better leader. But, you know, we weren't that good. I mean it just comes down to it."

CHAPTER 3

B.J. Johnson

B.J. Johnson is a legend in Texas high school football.

At South Grand Prairie High School in the Dallas–Fort Worth metroplex, Johnson became a bona fide star on the gridiron and one of the top wide receivers in the country. As is often the case with high school athletes, Johnson's first love was basketball. Though he hoped his hoop dreams would take him to the NBA, his football coach at South Grand Prairie High School, David Thompson, told him that football would be a better route for him. Johnson soon became a mythical figure in Dallas football circles as he lit up scoreboards every Friday night.

"I grew up playing basketball," Johnson said. "I wanted to be Penny Hardaway. That was one of my childhood idols. Coach Thompson came in one day to talk to me, and I remember Coach Thompson coming up and saying, 'You're not going to be a tall basketball player, but you can be a tall receiver.' He said I could play on Sundays if I really put my mind to it, because at that point in time I just played football just to play football because my friends all did. My best friend I grew up with that I always played basketball with, as kids I watched him play football for the first time, so I ended up playing football because he played football. Then I end up going to college to play football, and he ended up going to college to play basketball."

The 1990s were an up-and-down era for the Texas Longhorns. Scattered among a few strong seasons were mediocre finishes that saw a transition from John Mackovic to Mack Brown. While Brown was on the verge of ushering in a golden era of Texas football, Florida State was the national power everyone wanted to play for. Johnson was no different, and the Seminoles had a player he could see his own skill set in.

"Florida State and Peter Warrick," Johnson said. "That's what I wanted to do. At that point in time, Peter Warrick was everything to all of us. I mean, Peter Warrick—I can't remember who the game was against, if it was Tennessee or somebody—but he made like eight or nine people miss. I patterned my game in high school after him, acting like I was Peter Warrick. I just wanted to make everybody miss, plus I didn't like getting tackled, so I had to make them miss because I didn't like getting hit. So, you know, Florida State was the school that I wanted to go to naturally."

Perhaps Johnson would have never been a Longhorn if it wasn't for a pair of influential coaches who crossed his path. Legendary Dallas Carter head coach Freddie James, who was famously portrayed in Buzz Bissinger's book *Friday Night Lights*, was friends with Johnson's father. James encouraged Johnson and his father to attend camp in Austin, where Johnson ultimately met Texas wide receivers coach Darryl Drake.

"I didn't start loving Texas until I had to go down to a football camp," Johnson said. "They do their annual camp, and I went down. Freddie James, who used to be the coach at Carter—him and my dad were friends. And he said, 'Let's take him down to this camp.' So I went down to the camp. And I remember staying in the dorms right there on West Campus, somewhere between 22nd and 24th. I went down there and did the camp, and I met the receiver coach at that time who was Darryl Drake, and that's kind of what made me start liking Texas and having more interest."

Recruiting is often about relationships. Darryl Drake connected immediately with Johnson and provided him with an older Black mentor who had a fatherly influence. Though it was the late '90s, The University of Texas still had a tainted past when it came to race relations. The 1969 Longhorns were famous for being the last all-white team to win a national championship. Those feelings still lingered in inner-city Dallas, and it wasn't popular for African American kids to choose Austin. When Johnson originally signed with the Longhorns, his father, Willis, who served as a well-known DJ for KKDA 730 AM in Dallas, heard pushback from the community.

"I fell in love with Coach Drake," Johnson said. "There was something about him that was genuine and real. He reminded me like having a second father. And so that's kind of when I started looking at Texas, but I never grew up wanting to go to Texas ever. You got to understand from my dad's generation—my dad was a disc jockey right here for 30 years, and he got so much hell from me signing with Texas from the Black community. And so that's why we never grew up loving Texas. I used to love watching Mike Adams in early '90s—and he's now a big brother of mine—but other than that, Texas was never a school I watched that often. I remember seeing James Brown playing and having success, but that was just never the school I wanted to attend."

Mack Brown's presence at Texas started to heal relationships in the urban centers of metropolitan Dallas and Houston. Johnson was part of the first wave of Brown's rebuild, but he often had to confront that history. Whether it be meeting a member of the '69 team or sharing a bus seat next to legendary Texas head coach Darrell K Royal, Johnson wanted to be a part of changing the narrative at Texas.

"So it was either freshman or sophomore year—I think was sophomore year—when we lost 10–7," Johnson said. "But we lose to OU, and—Coach Royal is still alive at this point—Coach Royal rides the bus back with us. Out of everybody that sits on the bus, he sits next to me. Obviously I'm shocked. But I remember the whole time we just talked about all kinds of different things the whole three hours back to Austin. It was a great experience, man. I could personally see for myself that he had grown a long way from what he used to be known for and how he was viewed in our community. So just to see my dad get so much flak about his son going to a particular school whose history had a coach that moved in a particular way when it came to the skin tone of its players, and then his son is now riding a bus with that particular coach, right? It's just so ironic and funny. He was a great guy and a legend to me. Sometimes people are just a prisoner of their time. America and sports have always been progressing and evolving, but that was a tough thing for a lot of Black players, man. I'm not the only player whose family dealt with that or understood the notions and underlying tones that go along with going to UT and its history."

Johnson's relationship with Drake grew strong after their initial meeting. At that point Johnson hadn't met Brown face-to-face, but that would come later. Brown was known as "Coach February," which served as a backhanded compliment praising his recruiting skills while also pointing at his failure to win in big moments. At that time there was nobody in America who was better at going into a living room and closing a deal in recruitment.

"I would say probably sophomore or junior year we started engaging more after that camp. Then after, I went down and did a private workout with just me and Coach Drake, and then from there me and him started building a bond. That's when they started getting really heavy into recruiting me."

Recruiting rules have changed drastically in the last two decades. Home visits in the past were a free-for-all, with coaches pulling every trick in the book to monopolize a recruit's time and keep other schools out of the home for as long as possible. Johnson remembers a humorous story that involved Brown and Phillip Fulmer, Tennessee's head coach at the time.

"I remember this one night I was supposed to go to a basketball game at South [Grand Prairie]," Johnson said. "I was supposed to take Coach Brown to a basketball game, because at the time one of my best friends Ashley Robinson was getting recruited by the University of Tennessee. So [Tennessee women's basketball coach] Pat Summitt was always coming up to the school. Pat Summitt is sitting here having lunch with us, right? And so we're talking all the time, and I'm thinking, 'You know what? I'm going to get Coach Brown to come up here to school since you're bringing Pat Summitt.' So Coach Brown, Drake, and Coach [Bruce] Chambers get in town, and Phillip Fulmer from Tennessee was in town too. So apparently Coach Fulmer and their coaches got to the airport at Love Field first, and they saw Coach Brown's plane. So they knew they were in town. So Coach Fulmer comes over—and those were my top two schools, Tennessee and Texas. He clearly knew that Texas was in town. He literally stayed from like 6:00 PM to almost 11:30 PM. He wouldn't leave! So I didn't even get a chance to go to the game. I didn't get a chance to take Coach Brown and show him off like Ashley was doing. Then Drake is consistently and persistently calling my dad saying, 'What are y'all doing? What is going on? Why is he still in there?' So Coach Brown and Coach Chambers still joke and talk about this meeting all the time, but Phillip Fulmer was like, 'I'm not letting you come in this damn house,' and I mean he literally would not leave. We got to the point where he was just sitting on the couch, and we're just watching TV and not discussing anything."

When it came time to see schools for himself, Johnson and his father went all over the country. Before taking his five official visits during the fall of his senior season, Johnson saw several programs on unofficial visits during his sophomore and junior seasons. Johnson gave Texas a silent commitment before his senior season in high school but still wanted to enjoy the visit process. Seeing other schools only served to reinforce his decision, though a trip to Tennessee did catch his eye.

"I did a bunch of them," Johnson said. "I did a bunch of unofficial visits. So I went down to Miami. My dad took me to UCLA. We went up to Notre Dame. I saw several different schools unofficially, but secretly I went ahead and did a silent commit to Texas. So after my junior year I had told Coach Brown, 'Hey, I'm coming here, so don't worry about me.' So when we did that, I just wanted to enjoy the process. Then once I went through it, I really didn't even want to go anywhere else. I was kind of set. I was doing what I wanted to do, and I was happy. Tennessee was incredible though because I went and saw Tennessee and Notre Dame on my official visit in Knoxville. That was when Tee Martin, Jamal Lewis, and Donté Stallworth were still there. You know? Guys that were balling every Saturday. There was 107,000 people in the crowd. You got "Rocky Top," their fight song, being sung every 10 minutes. I mean the atmosphere was electric.

Then on top of that they had just won the national championship the year before—and taking that visit, that was my first time seeing 100,000 people in a stadium, and I was like, 'Yeah, I can do this for sure.'"

His official visit to Austin cemented the process completely. He was hosted by Texas quarterback and former five-star recruit Chris Simms, and he also met a pair of players who would become best friends to him forever. For Johnson, the family environment at Texas was unparalleled.

"I got a chance to meet Chris [Simms]," Johnson said. "Chris was my host on my recruiting trip. I met Kwame Cavil and Peanut [Richard Hightower], who ultimately became my roommate. He's now a coach for the San Francisco 49ers. So they also hosted me, and they took care of me for the weekend. You know, it was like it was already like a brotherhood that instantly started to form. Kwame and Peanut, to this day, those are my two big brothers.

"So Simms was my official host, and when he picked me up the first thing he did was take me to Peanut and Kwame's apartment. When I got there they brought me in with open arms and showed me nothing but love from day one. Kwame was getting ready to head to the league, and it was just a lot of positive encouragement, because, I can remember, Roy [Williams] went to his A&M visit, and the receivers there just left him alone. You know, it was like those guys didn't want him coming in and taking their jobs. We never felt that going to UT. It was just always a brotherly thing. So for us to pay it forward, we always returned the favor for recruits that we brought in. We did the same thing with Vince [Young]. It was always an atmosphere of family with Coach Brown and the whole staff, and we genuinely felt that during our recruiting trip."

Before the age of social media, it was rare for recruits to know others from across the state or country. Texas was also after Odessa Permian's Roy Williams and Klein High School's Sloan Thomas. Brown wanted to lock down the three best receivers in the Lone Star State. The three connected and started talking about the possibility of going to the same place and changing the face of the program.

"Me, Sloan, and Roy had been talking that whole time, and we probably did what kids won't do now—we decided 'let's all team up,'" Johnson said. "'I know we're all the top receivers in the country, but let's team up and go down there together to change the program.' Kids nowadays, they run from that. They don't want to go where all the same good guys are going. They just want to go somewhere they can do their own thing and get their numbers.

"Thinking back, I want to say somebody gave us phone numbers. We would talk to [Texas quarterback recruit] Chance [Mock]. I remember Roy and I had a chance to compete against each other once—we raced against each other junior year. That was the only year I ran track. We raced up in Lubbock against each other in the 100. That's when we first kind of met and started talking. Then, I want to say, we went to California to the Texas-California All-Star Game. That was the time when we got to kick it and got to know each other. I was hurt. I had messed up my ankle playing basketball at a local YMCA, so I couldn't play, and then Sloan had just had a scope on his knee, so he couldn't play. Roy was the only one that suited up."

Roy Williams is one of the more unique characters in Texas football history. A freak athlete at the wide receiver position who stood 6'3" and weighed 215 pounds, Williams was a unicorn as an athlete with the size of a linebacker and 10.3-second speed in the 100-meter sprint. For all the attention Williams garnered on the field, Johnson said he got an up close look at Williams off the field for the first time at the Texas-California All-Star Game, where Williams surprised everyone with a taste for a unique dessert that would later appear as a staple at the State Fair of Texas.

"So we all stayed in the same rooms at that event, and that's when the whole infamous story about Roy cooking the fried OREOs story came out," Johnson said with a laugh. "He's weird. He has hazel contacts for what reason? I don't understand this, and he fries his OREOs. That's what he used to do. Why? Who knows? I think he gets the opening kickoff return and gets hit pretty good, and—boom—he's done and comes out of the game. So neither one of us actually played the whole time we were out there, but that was the first time we got a chance to hang out. And then the rest of the summer before our freshman season, I mean, we all stayed together with Chris Simms. We went back and forth that whole senior year just talking on the phone. But we never got a chance to compete against each other when it came to football."

The three-star receivers kept in touch throughout their recruitment, but before the days of group texts and FaceTime, it was an old-fashioned three-way phone call that led to the trio finalizing plans to go to Texas. Playing with Thomas and Williams was one factor for Johnson, but the education at The University of Texas and the ability for his family to see him play also weighed in.

"Well, definitely the Texas-California game—we had already signed on signing day. But, I want to say, the end of junior year going into the season, we had just kept having phone conversations. I want to say we did a three-way call one time. We just kind of finalized it like that's what we were going to do. Because our whole goal was, is, we wanted to change, you know, what was going on in Austin. As a young recruit, you want to go wherever you can play early. That's not necessarily always the best decision for a kid. Just because you want to play early doesn't mean you need to play early. But we all thought that we had a chance to be able to contribute as soon as we got on the Forty Acres.

"Kwame wasn't coming back for his senior year, and they really just had Montrell [Flowers]. So that was really like our opening, where it was like everything just lined up. We just knew that this is probably the best decision for us, and it's a good school. At the end of the day, I mean, the opportunities that the school can do for you after football was also a factor. I had an ailing grandmother at the time, and I wanted her to be able to see me play. If I go play in the SEC, can she always watch me? I know if she lives in Texas, she could always catch the UT game. So, you know, a lot of those little factors is what ultimately went into that decision."

The biggest factor for Johnson was his relationship with Drake. That first relationship Johnson formed with the Texas assistant was the strongest, and Drake treated his three superstars like sons. Sadly, Drake passed away in 2019, but Johnson still keeps in contact with his family.

"It was literally Coach Drake," Johnson said. "At the time they had Simms, but I didn't know much about Simms. But they also had Opie [Major Applewhite]. I always heard about Opie. I just knew Coach Drake was a coach I could relate to and mature under. I had met so many different coaches. I had one coach lock me in an office at South Grand Prairie and offer me money. Another coach offered me money over the phone. I mean, I had met so many different coaches doing that, but it was like Texas never did that. They never offered me money or [a] vehicle or anything like that. Coach Drake was just such a genuine dude. Once we were all done playing football, it was still like family. We all called, call his wife Mom—Mama Drake to be exact—and since he passed, I always check on her. He coached Hines Ward at Georgia and guys like Larry Fitzgerald when he was in Arizona and was well respected—there was just a lot of guys he influenced. He was just a real down-to-earth kind of person and that was what really got me going and excited about attending The University of Texas. You don't deal with the head coach as a player—you deal with your position coach a lot. I would tell most kids to make sure you have a good relationship with your position coach. That's who you're with all the time. You're not with the head coach, and the position coach is going to make sure his job is good, so if you're doing your job, you'll be out there playing."

Brown may have been known as the best closer in college football, but his secret weapon in recruiting was his wife, Sally. Johnson said that the entire staff built a bond with his family that allowed his parents to sign off on the decision.

"My dad and Drake ended up forging a great relationship over the years until [Drake's] death," Johnson said. "They liked Mack. They thought Mack was a genuine guy. And obviously Mack would come in and he's good with his words. And then you got Sally. Sally closes the deal. She was Mama Brown, as I like to call her. My parents were fully on board. You know, my dad played football as a kid in high school, but during integration he ended up quitting because of all the fighting that was going on within his school growing up in East Texas in the late '60s. So his whole thing was—to me—was, 'I don't know the position that you're in, but I'm fully here to support you in whatever you want to do and the decision you want to make.' So it was never like, 'This is where you need to go. This is what you need to do.' He was like, 'Hey, I've never been here before, but I'm going to help you out along the way to make the best decision that you think is for you.'"

Johnson was on campus during one of the most tumultuous quarterback controversies in college football history. Applewhite was the veteran starter, but Simms sat behind him with tremendous promise. The battle raged back and forth, and lines were drawn in the locker room as players sided with their guy, but Johnson found himself in a tough spot. He was close with Simms and part of the younger group of players on campus, but he felt he would get more looks with Applewhite in the game. After an injury to Applewhite, Simms came in and lit up stat sheets, proving to be the type of passer every college in America thought he could be when he was recruited out of high school.

"First off I'm so glad we had such a tight-knit team the years I was there, 'cause it's real, man. Especially if you got the whole older class and the younger class scenario. The older guys are going to be with that kid and the younger ones [are] going to be with theirs. Then for us it was a lefty versus a righty. It was a lefty that threw the football hard as hell and was 6'5", and then there was the short guy that was a righty that threw you a nice little loaf of bread and very easy to catch. Most players won't admit it, but it's a real deal. Personally, off the field me and Simms were tight. That's my guy. I never hung out with Major once off the field. But on the field it was me and Major. That's my guy. So it was weird, like I would never advocate for Simms to come out *ever*, but I knew when Major got in—shit—I knew I was going to get some extra looks. So it's little things like that where you start to see that divide that can split a locker room. Whereas some guys were like, 'I know if Major gets in and Coach [Greg] Davis calls the play, and he don't like it, he'd be like, "We're not going to run that. This is what we're going to run.'" Simms was going to run it because that's just what he does—stick to the script—and there was nothing wrong with that. But with Major it's just like, 'No, I'm trying to win this damn game. That's not what we're doing.'

"And so when you start seeing that on the offensive side, some guys start leaning a certain way. It creates something that you don't want to create. You know, people always say if you got two quarterbacks, you don't have one. That wouldn't necessarily be true in our case. You know, we had two really damn good quarterbacks, and the problem was Major got hurt at the end of my freshman year at Texas Tech. So here comes Chris to fill in the next week against Kansas in the freezing cold. And then we had the big game against A&M and all of that, right? Our whole coming out party. Then me and Roy go stink it up in the bowl game and dropped some balls against Oregon that could have won the game, but Chris still played well. So then you take that into the next year, and Chris was still playing well. We ultimately go 11–2 that year, and Chris has a pretty good season. Then we get to the Big 12 Championship, and then it's like, 'Well, damn, what could we have done if Major was the quarterback all year?' Fair or not? But a question everyone asked themselves."

The battle really came to a head during the 2001 Big 12 Championship Game. The stage was set for Texas to make a national championship appearance after No. 2–ranked Tennessee lost in the SEC Championship Game. All the Longhorns had to do was beat the Colorado program they blew out earlier in the season, and they would face Miami for all the marbles. The Longhorns trailed 29–17 at the half, and Simms was replaced following a poor performance that saw him throw three interceptions. Applewhite replaced him, immediately throwing a 78-yard touchdown to Johnson. Applewhite rallied the 'Horns, throwing for 240 yards and two touchdowns, but Texas couldn't complete the comeback and lost 39–37. Texas fans never let Simms live it down, and the game remains a scar on a career that saw Simms leave Austin with a 26–6 record and rank as the second-winningest quarterback in program history.

"We beat Colorado 41–7 that year, and then we get to the Big 12 Championship. I don't know what happened still to this day," Johnson said. "I don't know. I can't say anybody was nervous, that's for sure. Maybe we were overconfident. We had already beaten them earlier in the season at home, and we had beat them the year before at their place. It was like we weren't worried about losing to Colorado. I remember like it was yesterday. Coach Brown came in and said, 'Hey, Tennessee just lost. The No. 2 team just lost. All y'all have to do is go out here and win.' We were so hyped right before the game—full of adrenaline—and then, man, we come in at halftime down and looking like someone stole our lunch money. I mean the mood just completely changed, and then we get so close at the end. There were a bunch of factors to why we didn't end up winning the game, as is in any game you compete at, but, you know, it is what it is now. But the way people treated Chris after that down in Austin was just horrible. To treat a 20-year-old kid like that just because we lost a football game. Sad and shameful. He won't go back to Austin to this day. He left as the one of the winningest quarterbacks in UT history and people hated him."

Johnson also got to see a quarterback controversy on the tail end of his UT career. He had come into college with Chance Mock. Mock had a strong promising career, but he was backed up by Vince Young. The former No. 1 player in the country was a legend at James

Madison High School in Houston, and he showed the type of dominant ability to take over a game. Though Young would eventually rewrite the Texas record books and post a 30–2 record en route to a national championship and finish as the runner-up to Reggie Bush for the Heisman Trophy, the beginning of his career was tumultuous. His unconventional passing style had several people wondering if he wouldn't be better off as a receiver, and no veteran was harder on him than Roy Williams.

While there were rumors that the older players at receiver didn't want to play with Young, Johnson had a close bond with him after hosting him on his visit and giving him a place to live when he first got to Texas. In the early days, Williams and Young constantly butted heads.

"So I can clear those rumors up," Johnson said, "we're all brothers to this day, and we still laugh about it. But Roy was tough on Vince. That's just the bottom-line truth. Sloan would say he was just a straight ass toward him. Roy knows it. Again, we laugh about it now, but in the thick of it there wasn't a lot of laughter going on. So, like I said, I helped recruit V.Y. Coach Tim Brewster, our tight end coach, said, 'We got this quarterback down in Houston. I need you to be his host, and I need you to make sure we get him.' When V.Y. first got on campus that summer he used to stay with me and Peanut. We'd go to 7-on-7 and workouts in the summertime, and he was still working on his arm. He had the funky throwing motion and all of that, but he was a pure baller. We would do warm-ups and go through the route tree. Balls would be high or in the dirt, and Roy would just be hard on him every time. We'd have to break them up because Roy would keep talking and antagonizing V.Y., and obviously V.Y. wasn't going to keep hearing it. So there was either going to be a fight or we are going to get back to work and continue to keep getting better. Some days V.Y. would be ready to leave early and be like, 'Let's go home, B.' We'd go home and he would go upstairs and shut the door. He didn't want to talk to anybody because he was so pissed. So he would always, I mean always, get into it with Roy. We would scrimmage the guys from Texas State, and they would come up, and we would do 7-on-7 against them, and they would see the arguments and the bickering. Roy would run a route, and the ball would be thrown over his head and/or behind his back. The thing about V.Y., though, was he was still young and raw. The talent was there and just needed some fine-tuning and confidence reassuring. I didn't have a problem with V.Y.—he was my little big brother—but for him and Roy, they did have a lot of issues in the beginning. He would always tease him and tell him he's going to be a receiver and he'd never play quarterback in college. That's what would always fuel V.Y. and get him really pissed off. But at the same time I do think it made him a little stronger and made him want to prove he could do it to a lot of people who thought he couldn't."

Even after entrenching himself as the starter during his freshman year, it wasn't a smooth transition for Young. The light switch didn't really come on as a passer until midway through his sophomore year, but Johnson wasn't around by that time. As the Texas offense moved more toward a ground-based read option attack that would eventually win Texas a national title and two Rose Bowls, the star receivers were relegated to blockers for Young and star running back Cedric Benson.

"My senior year we weren't catching anything," Johnson said. "We were just blocking. My senior year I led the team in pancakes. I had more pancakes than the linemen. That was when Vince was transitioning into the read option offense. We hated running 45 Q. We hated that with a passion, but 45 Q won the national championship."

For any football player at Texas, the annual rivalry game against Oklahoma is a highlight of the season. The 118-year-old rivalry is played on the second Saturday of every October with the State Fair of Texas in Dallas as the backdrop. The neutral ground situated almost equidistant to Norman and Austin often determines the fate of each team's season. Though Johnson went 0–4 in his career against the Sooners, the memories from those games are etched into his brain forever.

"My first memory of playing in the Texas-OU rivalry is pulling up in the parking lot," Johnson said. "I'm sitting on the bus. It's kind of cold, gloomy, and rainy. You look outside, and all I see is a bunch of older white ladies wearing crimson red. And as our buses are passing by to enter the Cotton Bowl, they're all just giving us the middle finger, yelling, and screaming with so much pride and hate. I was kind of like, 'Wow, that's what we do here?' I really couldn't believe it—I couldn't understand it—but now I understand it because of the passion of college football and the loyalty fans have toward their schools. It wasn't that they were giving us the finger personally, they were just giving it to Texas. That game—the years I was there—we just always had something go wrong. We always felt like we had the most talented team every year, but, like I said, there would always be something where it wouldn't go right. We as receivers always felt like Coach Davis, our offensive coordinator, called bad games. We always missed a lot of opportunities that we never could take advantage of, and they always did the same thing over and over defensively. They were just playing cover two sitting in zone, and we just could never figure it out as an offense for some unfortunate reason, but we always felt like we had a better team. We felt like we had the better defense, quarterback, and the better skilled players, but it didn't translate into wins."

Johnson finished his college career with 49 games played, 2,389 yards, and 16 touchdowns. He finished in the top 10 in all-time receptions, receiving yards, and receiving touchdowns at UT. Johnson suffered a serious tibia injury his senior season that plagued him and his draft prospects when he left school in 2003. He eventually caught on with the Denver Broncos for a short stint but never stuck around in the league due to ailing injuries. When asked if he would pick UT if he could do it all again, Johnson said he wouldn't think twice. His only regret was that he didn't leave college after his junior season.

"Absolutely," Johnson said. "My only regret that we always laugh about now is that we wish Roy would have declared earlier our junior year. So he waited until like the last hour to say whether he was coming back or if he was leaving for the draft. He came back because he wanted to win the Heisman. Well, needless to say, no one is winning that award blocking all year. Sloan and I give him a hard time about wrecking our draft options because he was selfish. Ha! But it's all love! It may be funny for us now, but if he would have just said he was coming back, I would have left. Based on the information given to me at the time, they had me rated right where [Texas A&M wide receiver] Bethel [Johnson] was. I was right in front of Bethel. And I always say if I could have left, I would have got drafted by the Patriots. Imagine that. Ha! And Bethel is known as Bethel "Two-Time" Johnson because he has two Super Bowl rings. That would be my only regret. Hindsight though, right? Other than that, man—I mean, the times that I had down there, the people that I met. I tell kids now all the time, 'Don't choose the school because you just love it. Choose it because what it can do for you in your life after athletics.' Going to UT, the things after football for me, personally, have been tremendous. Like the people and the connections. I mean, the current governor [Greg Abbott] went to UT. When I was at UT, we used to talk to the governor my freshman year who eventually became President [George W.] Bush all the time when we, when he was there at the facility. I would see Rick Perry when he was the mayor at the time. We both were going through rehab my senior year—he would be working on his knee, and I was always working on my tibia in the training facility. And now I'm in business with my family, and politics always plays a part with my dad's company. So, you know, the connections that I've gained from it have been tremendous. I could have gone to Notre Dame, but living here in Dallas, how would that have helped me? Maybe in Chicago, but living here, you know—if you go to Texas or if you go to A&M or go to SMU, that'll benefit you the rest of your life. You can only play football for so long, but you've got to work for the rest of your life."

Johnson never finished his degree, but he's working on completing it now. Just 20 hours shy of achieving his T-Ring, a ring given to student-athletes who lettered and graduated, Johnson has been incredibly successful in the business world. Johnson owns two businesses alongside his father, including a ready-mix concrete business and a public affairs firm that provides strategic support services in multiple cities. He also partners with Roy Williams as a cofounder of MVP Vodka, while also running youth camps with Sloan Thomas in conjunction with The University of Texas in Austin for the last 16 years. Amidst everything in his busy work schedule, Johnson is also raising a family. He just welcomed his third son, Justin Carter, last October, and his oldest son, Keylan, currently plays at Tarleton State University in Stephenville, Texas, while his middle son, Austin, is the glue of the family. Johnson was able to share his wisdom with Keylan when he was guiding his oldest son through the recruiting process.

"The biggest thing was, for him, is understanding how coaches move," Johnson said. "So like I told him, you know, he would always wear his emotions on his sleeve, right? And so if he's having a bad game, you can tell he's having a bad game. And I told him, 'You must stop doing that, because coaches see that, and coaches talk. Your position coach will meet with you in meetings, but then he's going to go back to the offensive coordinator and to the head coach, and then they're going to discuss what you're doing, how you're progressing, and where you should be and where you shouldn't be.' And so for him to understand that it's not just as simple as, 'I'm the best one out here.' There's a whole mixture of diverse factors that you must understand that goes into decisions on how guys get on the field and how that ultimately affects your chances to get to the league. Because you still got to go to school. Football is one of the sports where you have to go to class or you can't play. So understanding that dynamic and understanding that football can help be a starter to your life. There's a lot of guys that have made a lot of money at 21, 22, 23, where people don't make that until they're 35, 40, 45 years old. So if you really want this opportunity, take it serious and make it your life right now."

Though his football career is over, Johnson still wants to make an impact at the university he loves by continuing to host youth camps with his Longhorn brother Sloan at Darrell K Royal Stadium in Austin. The university's slogan reads, "What starts here changes the world." Johnson tries to put those words into action by encouraging campers to excel in more than just athletics. During the summer of 2020 the push for social justice reached colleges across the nation. UT players stood in protest of several university traditions with ties to racism. The biggest hot-button issue was the beloved school song, "The Eyes of Texas." Historians found the song's origins had ties to minstrel shows in the early 1900s. As an African American working to help move America forward, Johnson said his concern is helping the African American community become more of a presence at Texas. He hopes to achieve that goal with an endowment in the name of his former coach and mentor Darryl Drake.

"Right now what we're working on is trying to get an endowment done in Coach Drake's honor," Johnson said. "One of our goals is with our charity—we want to try and help get more African American kids get into UT. I know the current players were upset about the fight song and its [origin], but maybe that was a negotiating chip for a larger conversation to be had. We sing the song at our annual golf tournament—I don't care about that, honestly. What I truly care about is what you're actually doing for people and how you're changing their lives for the better. Our biggest thing is what can we do to get the numbers up at UT? When I was there we had 50,000 students and there were only about 1,100 African American students. We all knew each other because everyone came from the same high schools either in Dallas or Houston. So what we want to do is expand that footprint just a little bit more. That essentially is the core of our mission and what Sloan, Roy, and I are trying to work on vigorously to help affect change in our lifetime at our alma mater that gave so much opportunity to us."

CHAPTER 4

Quan Cosby

Quan Cosby never dreamed he'd be a college football star.

Growing up in Mart, a small central Texas town just east of Waco with a population of approximately 2,000 people, his biggest dream was playing for the hometown Panthers on Friday nights in the fall. The school's football team is a state power at the small-school level, with more 800 wins, 12 state championship appearances, and 8 state titles.

Cosby's life wasn't easy growing up. His father was incarcerated, and his mother did all she could to raise four boys while working several jobs. Cosby and his siblings grew up quickly, learning to cook and take care of themselves while their mother was away working. When he was 13 his home life fell apart and he was adopted along with his twin brother by friends of the family. Like so many other kids in similar situations, Cosby turned to sports as an escape.

While growing up as a young standout athlete, Cosby caught the attention of legendary head coach Terry Cron. Cron had already won a title at Bartlett and would go on to win at Mart and Commerce, accomplishing the rare feat of winning at three different levels of Texas high school football.

Cron had also coached some special talent along the way and knew what was needed to play at the college level. It wasn't long after Cosby arrived in high school that Cron let him know he had the potential to play at the next level.

"Football came first because my coach was Terry Cron," Cosby said. "Coach Cron actually also coached Plez Atkins and Claude Mathis. Both of those guys went on to play Division I. Claude was at Southwest Texas and Plez was at Iowa, and then [Cron] ended up just having a phenomenal career. A little bit early on, he was like, 'Hey'—he kind of started paying a little more attention to me even in middle school. And then when we got to high school, he was big in education. He said, 'I want you to take the good courses and ACT as soon as possible because I think you can play at the next level.' And, to be honest, I never really thought about it like that. About that same time, my oldest brother went to college and played college ball. So then it started—you know how exposure does—and I'm like, 'Holy crap, maybe I can do this. I always wanted to go to college. You know, I can't afford it, but maybe this will get it for me.' And so, really, that was kind of sophomore year when I became the quarterback at Mart. I was like, 'Hold on. I can actually make a future of this, at least to get to the next level and get my school paid for.'"

It's common at small high schools for top athletes to specialize in multiple sports. Cosby was the star quarterback on the football team, leading the Panthers to a state championship as a junior in 1999 and a state final appearance in 2000 as a senior. He earned the rare distinction of being a five-time All-State selection as both a quarterback and a defensive back.

Cosby was also a star in track and field, where he won state titles in multiple events, and on the baseball diamond, where he played outfield. Growing up close to Waco, Cosby befriended Baylor star and future Major League catcher Kelly Shoppach, thanks to a relationship with Shoppach's brother who coached at Mart. It was during his senior season that a future in professional baseball appeared to become a real option.

"My junior year I won state in the 100 meter and 200 meter and ran track," Cosby said. "About that time, Baylor was just down the street from Mart. Kelly Shoppach was there and his brother [Kyle] was, was actually a coach at Mart. So I befriended Kelly, and he heard I played baseball as well. He told me he was going to send some folks down there to see me. We ended up making it to the playoffs, and I had a really good few games. The weird thing about baseball, man— it's funny because the guy who ended up following me and scouted me, he saw me in football…. He saw me run track, and someone there told him I played baseball. He was from the [Los Angeles] Angels. And you go from one [scout] to like 60. And I was like, 'Whoa, maybe these people are serious about me playing a little bit of baseball,' because Mart is a football school, you know. We own that and most of the schools down here are like that. Although we have some amazing baseball players, football is king. So that's when I realized it, the more I started talking to them—and next thing you know, by the time I'm a senior I didn't have a lot of classes because I'd already taken care of business and started after lunch or during lunch or after school. I was going to hit, to take batting practice for guys, and going to throw and starting that whole process. So it was, it was pretty wild, and, of course, I had already committed to Texas at that time for baseball and football. So I went to a camp at UT, at Baylor, at Texas A&M, and I ran really good at all of them. From that point on, I was offered."

Before his baseball prospects took off, Cosby went through a traditional football recruitment. Mart became a common stop for the nation's top coaches who came in to see the dynamic quarterback who could take over games on his own. Growing up watching dual-sport stars such as Bo Jackson and Deion Sanders had Cosby looking out of state, but several of the regional powers would soon grab his attention. Though he ended up a Longhorn legend, Cosby didn't grow up dreaming of attending UT.

"Not at all," Cosby said. "Not even close. Honestly I wasn't a Texas fan until I chose Texas. I'm not going to say I was an Auburn fan, but I grew up liking Bo Jackson because he was a dual-sport guy, and then that morphed into Deion. Honestly if I say there's one school that I watched more than any of them, it was Florida State. Florida State was also the very first school I went to in recruiting, and it was awesome. Coach [Bobby] Bowden was still there, and he was phenomenal. He came to Mart and signed autographs for all 300 folks in my school and some people around town. So that was really my first choice, but at the same time that same year, Oklahoma beat Florida State in the national championship game in [2001]. Then my second trip was Oklahoma, and it was only four hours from home. I was very seriously considering them. Roy Williams [was] my host [at Texas], and me and Roy still talk monthly to this day. He's just such a good dude. Texas just being the flagship [university] and then Mack Brown doing Mack Brown things—I slowly but surely, in between him and Miss Sally [Brown], started falling in love with it. Honestly out of all of them, if I had to say, and I've told Coach Brown this—he was phenomenal in recruiting—but who recruited me probably better than anybody was [Texas A&M] Coach [R.C.] Slocum. Slocum was amazing, man, and College Station was only about an hour from our house. He came down when he wanted to, and he came to multiple games. He was super honest just like Coach Brown. Nick Saban at the time was at LSU, so it became apparent when those folks start coming to the house and visiting, and it was a pretty surreal, kind of fun moment for that process."

Cosby's twin brother, Quincy Cosby, went to Baylor on a football scholarship, and Cosby also had cousins at programs such as Houston and Missouri. Seeing those examples of family members reaching the next level gave a small-town kid hope that he could make it at the next level. With football on his mind, Cosby started making official visits in the fall of his senior year. The 2001 class was loaded with future NFL stars, including Michael Huff, Aaron Ross, Derrick Johnson, Cedric Benson, and Tommie Harris. The central Texas region was home to Cosby, Harris, and Johnson, and Cosby was able to grow close to several of them through recruiting trips to the common schools they were considering.

"You know what's interesting about our trips?" Cosby said. "Tommie Harris, who's still a great friend of mine, Derrick Johnson, and Cedric Benson—we all went on our first four trips together. We actually didn't talk to each other before to plan it, but it just worked itself out. We went to Florida State together, we went to Oklahoma together, we went to Texas together. I take that back—it was really our first three trips because I ended up switching mine and going to Baylor, and not everybody went to Baylor. But our first three trips— Florida State, Oklahoma, and Texas—we all went together. So we'd all go, and we'd have a good time learning about the schools, and, more times than not, we get back together, and we'd play dominoes late, talking about the trip, and we all pretty much kind of made a decision that we're going to Texas. Then in the end, three of the four end up going. I don't know how Tommie feels about me telling this story, but Tommie, in all of our opinions, wanted to go as well. But I don't know that Tommie's parents wanted him in Austin. They said it was a little too fast for him. We were fortunate in that we knew each other and knew of each other, but that led to the friendship that we still share today. And of course, you know—and Cedric is not with us—but Derrick is from the Waco area and I know his family like they're mine. Tommie is just supporting things in Killeen. We do a camp together. We've gone and kind of spoke about spiritual things together. It just led to some cool friendships."

During Cosby's first recruitment, Texas quarterback Chris Simms was his host. Simms was one of the biggest recruiting wins of the Mack Brown era, and he came to Austin as a heralded recruit. After a tumultuous career that saw Simms light up scoreboards and rewrite the record books while also ending up on the wrong end of a high-profile quarterback controversy, Simms left Texas and hasn't returned since playing there.

"Chris Simms was my host," Cosby said. "Chris was funny because he has such a weird relationship with Texas now, but he was all in at that point. I remember the quote he told me: 'Quan, if you don't choose Texas, I'm going to take that very personal.' It was a really, really, really good trip. And between him and the guys on campus, it was just good people, man."

When it came time for Cosby to make his decision, it would come down to Red River rivals, Texas and Oklahoma. Texas won out for Cosby for a few different reasons. The biggest was his desire to represent Mart at the flagship school in the state.

"Coach Brown just felt genuine," Cosby said. "You know, I think in the end it came down to Texas and Oklahoma. The weird dynamic about it all was I chose Texas because I went to Norman. Every other word was about Longhorn this and UT that. And, weirdly, they were the one, especially the second go-around—they have been five times in a row. But then I go to Austin, and they really didn't talk about Oklahoma. They knew that they were in my top three and all that good stuff, and they just said, 'Hey, they've had our number, but it's about the change.' Especially the second time. And so I think that there, that had certainly a lot to do with it. Being only one hour and a half from Austin and wanting family there. You grow up in a small town—you want your granny and you want your family to be able to come up and watch you. That was another huge factor—just being a Texas kid, man—the more I thought about it. Because it was truly about who I watched and who I wanted to kind of emulate. I'd have flown to Florida State in two seconds—Coach Bowden was pretty awesome too—but being a Texas kid, it was kind of going with the flagship. My senior year I dug in a little more into what Ricky did here and watching Roy and a lot of the different guys. A small-town guy actually walked down here, Jeremy Jones, and got some PT [playing time] on special teams. So seeing what he had did and how he had a real opportunity to do some things. And last but not least, track. I didn't go to Austin a lot as a kid but when I did, at Texas relays or at state, I just fell in love with the city. I was like, 'Man, I really do like Austin—especially old Austin.' It's funny. I call it old Austin now, but about 2000, or 20 years ago, it was a different place. Not that it's bad now because I still love it, but I just fell in love with it, and it had a big-city-with-a-small-town feel. I think it was kind of the best of both worlds for a Mart boy."

Texas assistant Bruce Chambers also played a big role in the decision. The former assistant coach and later head coach at Texas high school powerhouse Dallas Carter, Chambers was hired by Brown to help recruit from the inner-city programs in the Dallas–Fort Worth metroplex. Cosby's recruitment took Chambers more than 100 miles south of the heart of Dallas, but he was still able to play a big role in the decision.

"Coach Chambers is the man," Cosby said. "I know Mack gets all the love, but I promise you, as much as I love Mack, I don't know without Coach Chambers if I would have chosen Texas. He did that good of a job and always kept in great contact. Coach Chambers and I had a private dinner without Mack and without anybody else, and he was like, 'What are your thoughts?' I was—I told him what my bottom three was and the other schools in Texas I was considering, and it was cool how he put it. Baylor was one of them—I always threw them in the mix. He told me that Baylor was getting better. He actually predicted the [Art] Briles era before it got there. He said, 'They're putting money in their program—it's serious to them—and I, Quan I'm telling you, they're going to be better one day. The problem is it won't be in your time.' He said, 'If you go there, you know guys are going to double-team you, and you're just not going to be able to produce like you would at a school where you have more playmakers.' I was thinking that kind of makes sense. Then he talked about Oklahoma. He said, 'They've been killing us.' He said, 'They've had our number, but I promise—if you trust me, I promise you that's about to change.' We went 3–1 against them, and we were a fumble at the 2-yard line away from going 4–0, so he was pretty prophetic."

Cosby planned to split his time at Texas playing both football and baseball. He wasn't the first football star to also grace the diamond at historic Disch-Falk Field. The Texas program is one of the best in the history of college baseball. The Longhorns own the nation's best all-time winning percentage along with six national championships and six runner-up finishes.

Williams spent time playing baseball in Austin, and Benson was drafted by the Los Angeles Dodgers out of high school, where he played in the minors before quitting to pursue football full time. Cosby looked like he would be the next Texas star to play for legendary baseball coach Augie Garrido at Texas, but he chose the path that Benson didn't after being drafted in the sixth round of the MLB Draft in 2001. The opportunity to make money immediately and play at the professional level was too much to turn down. After a stint in the minors, Cosby decided to come back to try his hand again at college football.

"As much as I felt I wanted to play in the NFL one day, none of that is promised," Cosby said. "So now I have an opportunity to play a professional sport and, you know, play for a living. So that had a lot to do with it. Coming from Mart, Texas, and moving to Arizona and Provo and Iowa and Cali is a little bit different. My guardians always said that they didn't necessarily like that decision, because they're big on education. And I said, 'Hey, if I'm not in the show in five years, regardless of the situation, I'm going to come back.' A lot of people don't know that story, but that factored into it. And I missed football every single year, but I equally love baseball. As we were coming up on that fourth and fifth year, I was like, 'I'm going to keep my word and see if I can get back in school.' I didn't know how football worked or if I could even play the damn game anymore. But, certainly, Mack Brown told me when I chose baseball over coming to Texas, he said he was disappointed and happy for me at the same time. He told me, 'If you ever decide to come back, you have your full scholarship that I promised you before.' He honored that, and I hadn't touched a football in five years."

Cosby had to negotiate his way out of his contract to return to Texas. The Angels told Cosby he was part of their long-term plans as they were moving on from star outfielder Darin Erstad. Cosby reached the High-A level for the Angels' organization in Cedar Rapids, Iowa. He hit for a career average of .260 and stole 71 bases. Despite his future with the big club, Cosby stayed true to his promise. A big part of his negotiation was giving the team back a large portion of the money he signed for, but he felt it was time to move on.

Naturally Cosby would head right back to Texas, right? Well it wasn't that simple. While the Longhorns won quite a few games, their failure to win the big one loomed over the program and Brown. His "Coach February" moniker was a term of derision that mocked his ability to sign highly touted classes but fall short to Oklahoma's conference supremacy year after year. Cosby wanted to win a championship when he returned to college football, and he didn't know if that path existed in Austin.

Brown did get a call from Cosby, but Cosby also contacted Tennessee, where former Baylor assistant Trooper Taylor was. Cosby also contacted Bob Stoops at Oklahoma, and he even reached out to his hometown team Baylor to keep them in the mix as he had during his first recruitment. At 23 years of age, Cosby started over from scratch.

"I went through the recruiting process all over again," Cosby said. "I went back to Norman, and it all kind of reset itself. I went to Tennessee and Coach [Phillip] Fulmer ended up flying down to Mart. We had one of the best times ever in my living room. We laughed for three hours straight. My old man is a goofball, and Coach Fulmer loved him to death. Then I ended up going to Baylor and then I went back to Texas. So I kind of went through it all again. The next go-around was insanely cool because all the, the kind of various structured visits where you'd go to the library and then go to meet this professor. Just that whole recruiting rundown where they wear you out, and you can't wait to get out to 6th Street so that you can quit doing all the other stuff. I didn't really have that. I mean, I went to talk to coaches. I truly got to know the staff. They knew by then how important school was. So I knew what my major at least wanted to be, and then we went and talked to those specific people. And it was every school. It was so cool because I was treated almost [more] like a coach being recruited than I was a player. So it was a very different process."

While Texas had to get in the fight for Cosby a second time, Brown never took it personally. The Texas head coach approached it like a fresh recruitment, and it paid off for him. Just like many other recruits, Sally Brown also played a role in closing the deal.

"I told him I was going to talk to some other schools," Cosby said. "He's said he respected that. I told him, I said, 'Clearly my heart was with y'all before, so that puts y'all in the driver's seat.' Then I took my recruiting trip there, and Vince Young picked me up, and we had a real good conversation. Then we went to Mack's house, Miss Sally cooked, and that pretty much sealed the deal again."

Cosby's second recruitment had its own set of challenges. At 23, he had a different outlook than the teenagers the coaches were used to recruiting. His final four programs all understood and made accommodations that the normal prospective student-athlete wouldn't get.

"I came back, and I was like, 'So, Mack, I'm old now,'" Cosby said. "'Am I going to be in a dorm?' Mack said it was up to me. He said, 'You lived in five states. Why the hell would I make you live in [Texas athletic dorms], Jester?' It was that type of stuff where it was just that he was listening to me, though, and the conversation we had. I will be honest, Oklahoma had a better shot the second go-around, because Stoops and the same similar situation. I met his wife. He took me to his house, and it wasn't the rest of the recruits—it was just me. It was just different on that level."

Though Sally Brown's mashed potatoes might have sealed the deal in Cosby's heart, he left Austin without informing the Texas staff of a decision. Cosby went home to weigh his options and make a decision, but he didn't want to put the college staff recruiting him through an extended wait. In the end Sally got her guy in Cosby, and he made sure she was the first to know of his decision. Oklahoma's current head coach, Brent Venables, was an assistant for Bob Stoops at the time in Norman, and he didn't take the news as well.

"I wasn't going to wait," Cosby said. "The same respect they gave me not to send me through the same kind of BS recruiting stuff—I gave them that same respect. It was probably a couple weeks or maybe a week before signing day, and I called. The funny thing about just what I think of Miss Sally is I didn't call Mack. I said, 'Miss Sally, I wanted to let you know that I'm certainly choosing UT again,' and she's smiling and said, 'Yes.' I didn't realize this at the time, but Mack was literally right there. And I hear him say, 'I can tell about the smile—we might have good news.' Then at the same time—because, again, I'm older, so I think it's respectful—if you recruited me on that level, I respected it. I called every head coach and everybody that recruited me as well. Brent Venables ripped me a new one. He was like, 'I took it the first time because I thought you were young and just not mature, but this time I don't understand it. And, you know, you're just making the worst decision of your life.' He said some stuff I won't even repeat. I will say this, by the time we whooped them 45–35 my senior year, he said, 'You clearly, you made the right choice.

Y'all kicked our you-know-what for the last few years, and I wish you the best of luck.' So kudos to Coach Venables for being a man saying that."

Cosby was officially part of a 2005 class that didn't finish highly regarded in the recruiting rankings due to its size and recruiting industry misses on some players. The class packed some punch with players such as Colt McCoy, Jamaal Charles, Roy Miller, Jermichael Finley, Roddrick Muckelroy, and Henry Melton joining Cosby. The hit rate was incredibly high, and the class went on to a 56–7 record while at Texas.

The success of the 2005 group was magnified when one considers the players Texas didn't land. While McCoy would go on to be a Texas legend and one of the best college quarterbacks ever, he was seen as a consolation prize to five-star Louisiana quarterback Ryan Perrilloux, who made a signing-day switch to LSU. Texas also missed out on touted tight end Martellus Bennett, who went to Texas A&M. The class that was defined by its misses on National Signing Day went on to provide a foundation for the next run to a national title.

Since Cosby wasn't in the high school world, he didn't really know many of the players who would be joining him. And because Cosby had an apartment, he let incoming freshman Jamaal Charles live with him during summer workouts since freshmen couldn't be in the dorms until the fall semester started. The two bonded during that time and would both develop into key players for the Longhorns.

Cosby's original class still had some members on campus as well. As he bridged the gap between young and old, he felt comfortable in the middle of it. He would also meet Texas wide receiver Jordan Shipley. Another small-school legend out of Burnet, Texas, Shipley owned several Texas high school records and was a dynamic receiving threat. He and Cosby would grow into the most dangerous receiving duo in the nation by the time they finished their careers.

"The cool thing was there were still guys on the roster like still Aaron Ross and Cedric Griffin and all the guys who redshirted that I originally knew, outside of Derrick Johnson and Ced Benson, them who played as freshmen. A lot of the DBs and guys that [I was} originally going to come in with were still there. We all hit it off real well, and the things they did to get me back in shape was pretty phenomenal. Even my first time meeting Shipley—and he was a freshman when I was a senior—we ran together in a track meet. He asked if I remembered running in a meet in Glen Rose with eight guys, and there's just [a] little bitty white boy. I was like, 'Yeah, he was in green.' He was like, 'That was me, and y'all killed me.' We hit it off really well, so it was cool that all of the guys that were still there who knew a little bit about me before kind of told a story about how we knew each other and how they heard of me. It didn't take long, and, ultimately, you don't become a national championship team unless you have that culture. They said they were going to do whatever we need to do to get me ready."

Cosby wanted a chance to play for championships in college, and he didn't have to wait long. The Texas roster he joined capped off the previous season with a thrilling win over Michigan in the Rose Bowl. Vince Young ascended to the elite level of quarterback play and entered the year as a Heisman favorite. Cosby knew from the moment he arrived that the program had one goal in mind. Every team enters the season with the goal of winning it all, but those in the 2005 Texas program knew they were destined for greatness.

"I saw that Michigan game, and—that was honestly, with that level play in the game and the excitement—I was like 'I miss football.' I knew that a lot of guys were coming back, so I didn't think about natty [nationals] because, honestly, I didn't think I was going to play. I mean, that summer of '05, I've worked harder than I probably have my entire life to try to get in some kind of shape because baseball shape's a whole different monster. I mean that more about football shape. Baseball shape is pretty freaking easy. But seeing how they prepared, seeing the work they put in—we very openly talked about it. I was there for a couple of weeks. I was like, 'Wait, this is [something] different.' Our team meetings, the guys on the offensive side of the ball—Limas Sweed [Jr.] was a 6'4" teddy bear. Meeting Studds [Texas offensive lineman Kasey Studdard] and the other crazy ones, they worked on a championship level. So it wasn't very long when I was like, 'This is something different, and I need to really work hard to try to catch up to it.'"

Cosby's hard work paid off. He saw playing time early and contributed as a freshman with 15 catches, 270 yards, and two touchdowns. He'd also end up making a key play that would help Texas win the national title.

The words "fourth-and-5" live forever in Texas history as the Longhorns won the championship on a scramble from Vince Young with the game on the line. Though Cosby played sparingly, he was in on the last drive, and it's possible Young would have never had the chance to etch his name in college football lore without a drive-extending play from Cosby on third-and-12 earlier in the series.

"That was the last drive that Vince ended up scoring," Cosby said. "We did a little roll-out pass and needed 15 yards. It was four-down territory. So I caught it at about 8 and kind of ducked up under the safeties. His hands got up in the face mask, and we got that first down. It got us rolling, and that was the first drive after the fourth-and-2 stop, so it would have been tough to go right into needing a fourth-down completion. We never got fourth down again until Vince ran it in."

The Texas victory had special meaning for Cosby because of where it happened. The Rose Bowl in Pasadena, California, sat 35 miles from Anaheim, where many of Cosby's former baseball teammates were playing. The win even transcended international borders, as Latin-born baseball players in the organization who didn't traditionally follow American football were rooting him on. It's rare such a big choice is validated so quickly, but Cosby knew he was where he needed to be.

"Ironically, you know, going back to California and seeing friends there and all that stuff. I had some baseball buddies that were absolutely blowing me up. Shoot, I had Dominican guys calling me after, and so I got them into American football. Like I said, I made that decision with good old prayer. And I was like, 'You know? I don't know that the good Lord pays attention to football on this level, but this is pretty good confirmation that I made the right choice.'"

Following the Rose Bowl, a new era was ushered in at Texas. Young decided to leave school early and forego his final year of eligibility to declare for the NFL Draft. Young was selected at No. 3 overall by the Tennessee Titans, and the Longhorns would have to anoint a new leader.

To the casual observer, Colt McCoy was the least likely person to take the reins and continue the legacy at Texas. McCoy was the second quarterback in his recruiting class behind five-star Ryan Perrilloux before he defected, and five-star passer Jevan Snead entered the program in 2006 as a true freshman with hopes of being the next great Longhorn quarterback. McCoy was incredibly productive playing at the small-school level for Tuscola Jim Ned, but his time learning from Young as a redshirt freshman showed him how to prepare for the role.

Cosby was detached from the Perrilloux saga but followed it as closely as he could. Though he knew McCoy as a quiet freshman, he started to see flashes of his brilliance as McCoy competed alongside Snead for the right to replace Young.

"I kind of wasn't a part of it but knew every level of the Perrilloux stuff," Cosby said. "And then you bring in Jevan Snead. Jevan Snead was from Stephenville with Art Briles. They won so many state championships. And, you know, it's a five-star guy. He had height, he had decent speed. He could throw it a country mile. Watching them prepare on that level—and watching them compete on the level that they did in the post-Vince era—it was insane. It was wild to see, and Colt didn't start the year as a starter, you know. Snead was going with the ones and, and Colt just stayed at it. And it wasn't very long before Colt then was going with the ones. I take that back. Colt did, but it was split. It was almost like the stuff you see now. It was split, and Colt just didn't make a lot of mistakes. He took care of business. He studied hard. He had learned from Vince, and he put that extra time in. He didn't throw the same ball he threw by his junior or senior year that he did his freshman, but he could spin it. So seeing what his skill set was very early and knowing work ethic, I had a bias to him because he was another 2A guy. The way he led on that level, he always had it in him, and we saw it pretty early."

McCoy was a four-year starter at Texas. Though he worked through managing the offense in his first season, McCoy started to come into his own as a passer. Shipley was a childhood friend of McCoy's, as their fathers had been college roommates. While that friendship produced plenty of big plays for the Longhorns, Cosby and McCoy became the top duo in Texas history. The former 2A stars were playing on the highest level of college football, and Cosby's knack of getting open combined with his past as a quarterback helped to foster that relationship.

The other major factor was a change in offensive philosophy. Offensive coordinator Greg Davis featured Young in a spread read-option offense that was 70-to-30 run-to-pass ratio. While McCoy had the running ability to keep that element in the offense, his precise passing style allowed the Texas offense to open up the passing game more. As the Texas offense became more of a spread passing attack, players like Cosby and Shipley started to blossom.

"When he started, we got along pretty good," Cosby said. "I had been a quarterback back in the day and always thought a little bit like one. We'd have those conversations, so it all kind of worked itself out from that standpoint, especially our junior and senior year. Sweed was there Colt's freshman year, and me and Ship would kind of move all around. We also started throwing the heck out of [the] ball. We'd throw it a good amount when Vince was there, but I'd say that it was four or five times more when Colt [would] start taking care of business."

Cosby gained a bigger role in the offense as his career went on. In his sophomore and junior seasons in 2006 and 2007, he combined for 1,205 yards and seven touchdowns. As the offense started to click under McCoy late in 2007, Texas was primed for a huge year in 2008. Though the Longhorns would reach a No. 1 overall ranking and be on the hunt for a national title, nobody expected much from Texas entering the season. Cosby and his teammates saw what national title preparation looked like with the 2005 team, and he knew they had something special in 2008.

McCoy completed 77 percent of his passes for more than 3,800 yards and 34 touchdowns, while adding 561 yards rushing and 11 touchdowns on the ground. The addition of Will Muschamp to run the defense was also a huge boost to a program that had struggled on that side of the ball in 2007.

"From our standpoint, with [Brian] Orakpo and Roy Miller, we had a really good group of kind of core leaders. And the way we work was very, very similar to what we saw and all of us were on the team, or at least close to it, when we won the natty. Some guys had redshirted. I played, you know, Colt redshirted. So we knew what it took. We were throwing the ball way more. I think by the end of the season it was close to 70 percent completions for the entire year, which is why he was in contention for the Heisman. We took it pretty serious, and we knew how good we could be. Coach Muschamp was a huge addition. He got the best out of our guys like Orakpo, Roy Miller, and Sergio Kindle, and we had a good defensive back group."

The Longhorns started the season 5–0 and firing on all cylinders, winning by an average margin of 47–11. The middle of their schedule featured one of the toughest gauntlets in Texas history as the Longhorns faced four straight top-15 matchups with three of those teams in the top 10.

"It was a loaded Big 12," Cosby said. "Missouri was top 5, Oklahoma was top 5, you know, Texas Tech was top 5, Oklahoma State was like top 11 or something. Kansas, even back then, was winning Orange Bowls. We knew we were semirespected coming in, but once we went through that gauntlet—and should have been undefeated during it, but we all got hurt during the Tech game."

The Longhorns rolled into Dallas for the annual Red River Shootout and stunned top-ranked Oklahoma with a 45–35 win. Cosby recorded nine catches for 122 yards in a game where the Oklahoma defense couldn't find a way to stop the dynamic passing attack of the Longhorns. Texas went on to a No. 1 ranking and beat highly ranked Missouri and Oklahoma State teams over the next two weeks.

A Halloween matchup against No. 6 Texas Tech loomed large as the Longhorns looked to emerge from the rigorous schedule unscathed. In a game where everything went wrong in front of a rowdy crowd in Lubbock, Texas overcame injuries and turnovers to take the lead late in the game. With several key contributors out, the Longhorns looked like they would get out of Lubbock alive until Graham Harrell hooked up with Michael Crabtree for a game-winning Texas Tech touchdown as the clock was winding down.

That loss knocked Texas off track from their goal of playing in the BCS National Championship that year, and Cosby noted that the injuries in that game really hurt them.

"That's the thing about the Tech game," Cosby said. "Everyone talks about the Crabtree play, but I only played two plays that game. Orakpo didn't finish that game. Roy didn't finish that game because they were chop blocking all day, and it wasn't getting called. We had so many injuries that game. It was crazy."

The Longhorns went on to finish the season at 12–1 and had an outside shot of playing in the Big 12 Championship with a chance to go to the national title game against Florida. Though Texas beat Oklahoma head-to-head on a neutral field, a three-way tie between Texas, Oklahoma, and Texas Tech caused controversy because of the conference's tiebreaking rules. Head-to-head wins weren't taken into account, and the top-ranked BCS team would get the nod. Oklahoma edged out Texas in the polls, sending a disappointed Longhorn squad to the Fiesta Bowl to face 10th-ranked Ohio State.

In a back-and-forth game against a loaded Buckeye program, the McCoy-to-Cosby connection paid off for the final time as the Longhorns drove the length of the field, and McCoy found Cosby on a slant with 16 seconds remaining to pull out a 24–21 victory. Cosby's final college play was punctuated by a leap into the end zone that was flagged for unsportsmanlike conduct, but Texas would go on to win and send the kid from Mart out in style.

Cosby wasn't supposed to get the ball on the game-winning play, but Ohio State gambled with a heavy blitz package that opened the middle of the field. With a quick check at the line, Cosby leapt into the Longhorn history books.

"You know, the call was changed because they sent an all-out blitz," Cosby said. "And they did that blitz like three times during the game. The first time they did it was right before the half, and I guess that was kind of their tendency, depending on who they were playing. And then Colt threw the ball to Brandon Collins. Brandon thought he's about to get knocked out by that linebacker that popped out, so he kind of folded and missed it, and Colt and I had a little conversation about that. And I said, 'We already watched film on this. We said if they, if they do this—if they go zero—we're going to kill them.' And they, they did it again early before that time and they end up actually getting to Colt. But then that third time he saw that they showed their cards a little bit too early. By the time I looked at Colt, he had already given me the slant signal. I think I had a vertical originally, and we saw that all the way, and we were all over it. It was successful for them twice, so it makes sense. We did what we talked about in watching film before and it worked. Then the refs decided to call the stupidest penalty on the planet. It worked itself out. We talk about that time and why we were so good—I dove in not knowing that Malcolm

Jenkins wasn't chasing me. We got the penalty on the kickoff, and Roy and Rak [Orakpo] both came to and told me they had my back. If you go back and watch that game, they only went two plays because there was 16 seconds left. The first play, it was half sacks by Roy and Rak. That's the leadership we have, and that was what was so cool about and so special about that team."

Cosby's senior year was one for the record books. In 2008 Cosby recorded 92 catches for 1,123 yards and 10 touchdowns. He left Texas as the second-leading receiver in career receptions with 212, the third all-time receiver in yards with 2,598, and the fourth all-time receiver in touchdowns with 19.

Cosby also contributed heavily on special teams with a program-record 73 returns and a program-record 1,731 return yards. His 4,701 all-purpose yards rank at No. 6 all time. Cosby would go on to play in the NFL after being signed as an undrafted free agent with stints at several clubs. When he left Austin he knew that his teammates were on the verge of reaching their goals of a national championship in 2009. He hated that he couldn't be a part of the next step.

"I was sitting there going, 'Man, is there something I can do?'" Cosby said. "'I want to play with this team one more year.' And, honestly, me and Ship were so close. I was like, 'I want us to go out together. What we could do together would be pretty special.'"

After his NFL career was over, Cosby returned to Austin and took a job with the radio broadcast crew as a sideline reporter for Texas games. Cosby also took a job in commercial insurance, where he worked during the day.

Cosby left the radio job last year and stays in touch with the program as much as possible. As the team struggles through a forgettable decade,

Cosby hopes for the days when the once-proud program can reach the heights he saw while in Austin.

"I want UT to be really good again," Cosby said. "So it's cool—just being around UT is certainly something special to me and my family. Our era was special. The family perspective that we had during that time is why it's biweekly or weekly that we're chatting and keeping in touch and supporting each other in all sorts of ways. A lot of my boys, they live in Austin. I tell a lot of recruits, 'If you're thinking about us or Alabama or the next school—especially once we start rolling again—I don't know a lot of Bama guys who move back to Tuscaloosa. Honestly, most of them move to Austin or Dallas or Houston. The beauty and luxury of going to UT is you're back at your spot and there's so many memories and good times, and so it's pretty cool.'"

CHAPTER 5

Fozzy Whittaker

Foswhitt Jer'ald Whittaker was born in Houston, Texas, on February 2, 1989, to Foster and Gloria Whittaker. The youngest of three boys, Whittaker's name was a compromise reached by his parents. Foster always wanted a son named after him while Gloria was against that, so the two decided to put together something new using elements of Foster's first and last name.

While his family still calls him Foswhitt to this day, he's widely known as Fozzy Whittaker in the sports world. The nickname he earned from his older brothers, inspired by the Muppet Fozzie Bear, became famous enough to stand alone without his last name. Fozzy was a much easier name to pronounce, and it became commonplace among teachers, coaches, and peers. For Whittaker that was just fine, considering how badly his name had been butchered throughout his early years.

"My oldest brother actually was the one who called me that nickname probably since I was the age of 3 or 4 or somewhere around that time frame," Whittaker said. "I'm not quite sure where he even got it from. I'm assuming it was probably from the Muppets. He might have just said, you know, that's an easier name to say than my first name.

A lot of teachers would mess up my first name—they would see that, and it would get butchered. Man, I've heard so many different variations of my name, including my last name—a lot of people think the extra 'T' in my last name turns it into a completely different name. Whenever my brother started coining the term 'Fozzy,' for me, it just stuck. It made saying my name out loud for teachers a lot easier. And so ever since then I've stuck with it, just because I'd rather people say Fozzy as my nickname than people mispronounce my actual given name that my mom and dad gave me."

Whittaker played several sports growing up, but he grew a deep love for football. When he reached Pearland High School, it didn't take long for Whittaker to establish himself as a high school football force. Playing in the southeastern Houston suburb, Whittaker exploded onto the scene as a sophomore, posting 1,335 yards on the ground with nine touchdowns on just 175 carries. Now officially on the map, Whittaker started to receive mail from several schools indicating their interest in his talent.

"It was probably toward the beginning of my junior season," Whittaker said. "I was getting a little bit of traction. I had played varsity after my sophomore year or during my sophomore season, and I had kind of a coming-out party in my sophomore season. In my junior season I was the main feature back and was able to get a ton of opportunities and exposure. I think after that junior season it really started to pick up from a recruiting standpoint. That's whenever all of those interest letters will get sent out to gauge your time and your weight and your height. I just started to get that initial interest from colleges from all over that just started sending me some of their questionnaires for me to fill out. So, I would say, pretty much the beginning of my junior year was the start of whenever that recruiting process started to ramp up. And I think that's whenever I started to realize that I could be good enough to play D-I football."

At first, programs such as Baylor, Houston, Kansas State, and Oklahoma State recruited him heavily, along with Ivy League program Columbia. Later in the process he'd hear from some of the bigger football programs in the region, and Texas would eventually win him over. Despite growing up in Houston, Whittaker was a Miami Hurricanes fan as a kid. The Canes were one of the best programs in college football in the late '90s going into the early part of the 21st century, and Whittaker dreamed of playing for "the U."

"My favorite school growing up was actually Miami," Whittaker said. "I loved the U— the University of Miami had Larry Coker as the head coach at that time—especially in that 2000, 2001, and 2002 era. You got Ken Dorsey. You had every running back imaginable on that same squad. Obviously you go and look at people that produced in the NFL, and how many first-round draft picks came from that '01 national championship team? My favorite player was Sean Taylor. Then him coupled up with Ed Reed and Andre Johnson, it was a phenomenal team. Ironically, my older brother Curtis, his favorite team was Florida State. And so we always had an in-house rivalry between Miami and Florida State whenever they played each year. That was my team growing up, but I always watched Texas, especially whenever Ricky [Williams] was there. And then once V.Y. went there, it was a no-brainer, definitely, to watch. Then you see good talent like Ced B[enson]. Jamaal Charles going there kind of helped influence my decision to go to Texas, as well, once I got in high school, but Miami was my school of choice whenever I was growing—middle school, junior high, through there. I was [a] Miami fan."

It didn't take long for Texas to see Whittaker and open the lines of communication. Defensive line coach Oscar Giles was one of the coaches Brown tasked with recruiting the greater Houston area. Giles and running back coach Ken Rucker helped secure the swift runner down the line.

"Oscar Giles was the very first person that I had contact with," Whittaker said. "O.G. was the one that recruited the Houston area. He had obviously recruited people that I played against and people that I knew. Look at a guy like Chykie Brown—that was a guy that went to North Shore High School. I played against him two years straight [in] the playoffs. Another guy named Scott Derry—who actually went to my same high school at Pearland, who Oscar had contact with—he played middle linebacker at Texas. I look at guys like Jamaal Charles, who also was in the Houston area and played running back at Port Arthur Memorial who we played my freshman year in high school. I talked to a couple of those people and just asked him, you know, what Coach Giles was like, what The University of Texas was like, and really just seeing, you know, their perspective on who he is as a recruiter. Really that was my first person that kinda put me on to what The University of Texas was like. The people that he had already produced on the defensive line, that was amazing in my mindset. Then I got introduced to Coach Rucker—Ken Rucker—who was the running back coach at that time, and both of those guys played an important role in me basically committing to The University of Texas."

Mack Brown was an innovator when it came to recruiting. The Texas head coach constantly created new trends for other schools to follow. One example was their Junior Day event. This typically happened in February of the upcoming class' junior year, right after the previous class had signed. Today every school in the country has some sort of event, if not multiple events, that do the same, but Brown would make it special and send out a large portion of his offers during the event. To Brown, offering a prospect in person fostered a special moment for the coaches and the players. Whittaker was offered during his junior day visit.

"They typically didn't offer people unless they were in person," Whittaker said. "Coach Brown never sent an offer until I was there on campus with junior day. I got to speak to him in person. I got to talk to him in person as well as the rest of the staff and the other members that were a part of the Texas family. [Assistant director of football operations] George Wynn was huge in that component as well. But they didn't send out any offers until I got there in person on Junior Day. Whenever I got that offer I was stoked. I was extremely excited. It was something that I had always had Texas in high regard—I talked about Miami being the team that I originally loved—but whenever they fired Larry Coker, Texas [became] my favorite school. I've always been a Texas fan. I just loved Miami more at the time that I was in middle school, but when I was getting recruited, Texas was my top choice. And so getting an offer from my top school on Junior Day was really, really cool."

Texas had no problems recruiting at that time. Whittaker's 2007 class started their recruitment processes seeing Texas win a national championship in 2005. Though 2006 didn't result in a title win, the trajectory of the program was on an upward trend. Because of their status as a program, Brown could get anyone he wanted. The 2007 class was ranked No. 3 nationally and Brown landed 17 of 24 signees before the Fourth of July. In a class that included five-star prospects Tray Allen, John Chiles, and Curtis Brown, the group also had Whittaker, Earl Thomas, Keenan Robinson, and Cody Johnson. Whittaker didn't wait long after getting the offer to make a move.

"Up to that point I only had two offers," Whittaker said. "One was from Oklahoma State and the other was from LSU. Both had offered me over the phone. Whenever I went to Junior Day at Texas, and then Mack Brown kind of made the speech of, you know, 'We only offer people in person because we want it to feel very personal. We want that acknowledgment that hey, you know, you're going to be a part of this family if you commit with us.' I took that to heart as something that I truly loved about what Coach Brown did, because he did something different that those other two programs at the time, they hadn't done. It didn't make me feel like I was just a recruiting number. It made me feel like I was actually wanted from the standpoint of I'm willing to meet you face-to-face before I even give you an offer. That just was a little different style or a different way of doing things. Ultimately what came down to me committing to The University of Texas was how they used Jamaal Charles. That was a guy that we played against in high school, so I saw what type of style runner he was. I saw how they were utilizing the spread. And then I saw people like Jamaal Charles getting an opportunity as a true freshman to be able to play in the national championship game and throughout that entire season making a huge impact for the team. Another guy was Ramonce Taylor. He was used all over the place on the field. R.T. was a Swiss Army Knife for that offense, and Greg Davis knew how to utilize him to the best of his advantage. So I saw those two guys and that made me really want to go to University of Texas because I feel like I could have played in a similar role or a similar fashion into the way that they were doing things. I really appreciated that aspect of how they allowed young guys to play and how they allowed guys to play multiple positions and just be able to make plays. I wanted to be able to play, as well, in state—I wanted to play closer to home so that my mom could be able to make the, make the games. She could see them and drive to them and not have to worry about, you know, driving too far or having to catch a plane ticket for every game. So that played a huge factor into where I played as well."

Whittaker was raised most of his life by his mother. His father passed away in 1992 from lymphoma, leaving Gloria to raise three boys on her own. The chance to stay close to home was huge for Whittaker, but it was a big relief for her as well. The decision paid off, as Gloria never failed to be at a game he played in.

"My mom helped raise me and my brothers basically by herself for quite some time," Whittaker said. "That's been an amazing point for her but at the same time a huge burden because she's had to do it all alone. Whenever she found a way to support me, she would. Whenever I say found a way—she came to every game, home and away. And that was all the way through high school and all the way through college. That was all the way through my professional career. That was unless I didn't play. If I wasn't playing, like after I got hurt in college, then she didn't travel to the away games. She was still going to the home games, but she didn't travel to the weekends because I wasn't playing, so I told her save her money."

Like so many others who played at Texas during this time, Sally Brown made a big impact on Whittaker's family. Sally took in every player as if they were her own sons, and it helped ease the worries of parents sending their kids off to the big world of collegiate athletics. Gloria loved Sally from the moment she met her, which helped to smooth the transition.

"She definitely was on board with that decision of going to UT," Whittaker said. "She loved Miss Sally. Sally was, honestly, one of the biggest reasons why she was comfortable with me going to The University of Texas, because she acted as a mother to all of us. She would take care of us. She would cook for us. She made cookies before every game. It wasn't just Miss Sally. Coach Rucker's wife, Miss Ruck, she took care of us as well. It just was that family type atmosphere and environment that allowed [my mom] to feel safe that her son was all the way out in Austin a couple hours away but still getting taken care of. That's what kind of sold me as well on Texas in general, was just how much of a family environment and atmosphere was created from Coach Brown and Miss Sally Brown whenever they were there."

Whittaker made the decision to graduate high school in December and enroll at Texas in January with hopes of making an impact in spring practice and getting a head start on college life. He was joined by several players in the class, bringing a huge group of true freshmen in a semester early. Just a few years before, freshmen weren't even showing up to campus until fall camp started, but by this point it had become common for athletes to enroll in the first semester of summer school in June to start the process of working out and adjusting to college life. The jump to graduating early was another big one, but Whittaker had someone already on the Texas roster to show him the way.

"What Coach Brown used to do is have a panel of players on junior day," Whittaker said. "So all the recruits are in the team meeting room and all the players that he had on the panel—it was like five players typically, like five or six players—they're on this panel. There's an open period where the recruits and parents are able to ask questions. Then there's a period where the coaches and everybody on staff is out of the meeting room, and it's just recruits and players. Just having that access to be able to reach out to the players on a more personal level without having the coaches in there feeling like they have to monitor the conversation or have to control the conversation was really cool from that aspect. Sergio Kindle was a guy that had graduated early, and he enrolled early in the spring of 2006. I had a conversation with him. I had asked him a question about what it took to graduate early and what all you needed to do. I asked him then how was he adjusting to college life after he's technically supposed to still be in his second semester of his senior year. So after he answered those questions, I realized, you know, that could be a possibility for me. I was ahead in my classes already, as far as math, in English, and history. I had a ton of my credits already lined up. All I had to do was take the second semester of English 4 over the summer, and that would allow me to graduate early. So I didn't have to change too much of what I was already doing in order to graduate early. I thought it'd be a great decision to just go ahead and enroll early like Sergio Kindle did and basically get a leg up on learning the offense, getting acclimated to what it was like for the college life, understanding the academic side of it as well, and then being able to just get more time to adjust to what was going on and try to make an impact early in the spring. I thought all those were a much greater benefit to me than going to my senior year and then waiting to join in the summer."

Other schools tried their best to pry Whittaker away from his commitment to Texas, but the young man who always seemed to have wisdom beyond his years really showed that by approaching the decision-making process as thoroughly as possible. Whittaker was sold on Texas, but he also wanted to make sure he was giving his high school teammates everything he could as they made a push for a state championship.

"Once I made the decision—and this was a conversation that my mother and I had—she said she was going to support wherever I went," Whittaker said. "She did love Texas, but she said, 'Wherever you go, you know I support you. I'm going to get there, and I'm going to go to all the games regardless of wherever it's at.' She said, 'Once we do make the decision, make sure that's what you want to do and that's where you want to go.' So that, that's really what took me that week-and-a-half-or-so time that I spent trying to decide if Texas was the right spot for me. I just kept coming back to the same thing: I wanted to go to Texas and I wanted to be in Austin. I spent that time just eliminating all doubt. And it was something that I wanted to do personally, but at the same time, I wanted to basically close my recruiting so that I could focus on my senior season and trying to win a state championship. I didn't want to have to deal with questions all the time. I didn't want to have to go into spring ball talking about, you know, this and that, because I think it would have taken away from what our team was trying to do. I didn't ever want to make it about me personally. So once I committed, man, I was committed, and I just was all about getting Pearland High School to the state championship and hopefully winning a state championship. It was, it was a done deal once I committed to Texas, so that was my mindset."

Whittaker's dedication to his high school team almost paid off. The Pearland Oilers reached the state semifinals before losing to the Austin Westlake team that had future NFL stars Nick Foles and Justin Tucker. Westlake would fall short of a state title the next week, losing to Southlake Carroll, but Whittaker was pleased with the effort his team put in. He finished his high school career as the sixth all-time leading rusher in the history of the 5A classification in Texas, which served then as the biggest classification in the state. Whittaker's 5,717 yards and 51 touchdowns were exciting numbers for Texas fans dreaming about his future. Despite playing arguably the best high school competition in the country, Whittaker arrived in Austin and realized the college game was a completely different level when it came to the tempo of the game.

"The biggest adjustment is definitely the speed of the game," Whittaker said. "There were people like Brian Orakpo, Sergio Kindle, Frank Okam, and people like Roy Miller who played on the defensive line and linebacker position, and they were running almost as fast as me. That's when I was like, 'There's a whole other level to this.' That was the biggest adjustment. Obviously a ton of people in high school could reverse field. You could take a toss play and run straight to the sideline, and then cut it up and get positive yardage. Whereas once I got to Texas, it was like there's no getting to the sideline unless somebody messed up on defense. If they're in position, there's no way you're just going to outrun the defensive end or the outside linebacker. So that was probably the biggest adjustment that I learned, and I learned that early in spring ball. That is why I wanted to get there, so I could adjust faster."

Whittaker redshirted his freshman year after practicing in the spring. The Longhorns were set in the backfield with Charles, who ran for more than 1,600 yards as a junior in his final year at Texas. At that time the NCAA rule stated that one snap on the field would comprise an entire year of eligibility for a player. That rule changed in 2018 when the NCAA ruled that an athlete could play in four games without losing that eligibility. For Whittaker, his decision to sit that year out allowed him to learn from one of the best in the game.

"I think redshirting was the best decision I ever could have made," Whittaker said. "It gave me an opportunity to sit behind Jamaal and really see what goes on. And obviously I'm still in the same meeting room, but it kept my eligibility. I would have lost my eligibility just by playing one snap…. It would have been phenomenal to be able to get some experience without losing that eligibility. Redshirting was the best decision that I could have made. Just seeing how that season played out—seeing how, you know, Jamaal handled himself and carried himself, and then obviously he had a unbelievable season rushing. I want to say he had like 1,600 yards rushing that year. It gave me an opportunity to see what it took to even just be a third-round draft pick. He did all that and still was a third-round pick. So that, that was an eye-opening experience just seeing that he was a third-round prospect, right? Obviously if you redrafted him, he would be much higher with what he did in the NFL once he got there, but that season that he put together kind of put him as a third-round pick. Now he was in a loaded running back class that year too. But at the same time it just was like that gave me the insight to see, 'Okay, he did this, he did this, he moved this way on this play. You know, he pressed the hole right here, and this netted him this amount of yards. This is something that he did. Okay—boom—I can take that and start applying that into my game to see how this offense can start turning into my offense if I'm ever the feature back.' So it was just great sitting behind him and learning there."

The transition from Vince Young's teams to Colt McCoy's teams wasn't always smooth. In 2007, McCoy's sophomore season, Texas finished 10–3 with a 5–3 conference record that saw them land in fourth place in the Big 12. Though they ended the season on a strong note, defeating Arizona State in the Holiday Bowl, nobody expected much from the Longhorns coming into the 2008 season. Texas would go on to reach a No. 1 overall ranking that year and would come one play away from a likely national title berth. Though many people couldn't see it, Whittaker said the team felt they were destined for greatness heading into that season.

"That was just the expectation of being at Texas," Whittaker said. "'This is Texas' was what we used to always use, kind of, as a motto. We do this because this is Texas. We've got to represent the state, we've got to represent our conference, and then we've got to represent what we stand for. A lot of the guys were from Texas. There were a few out-of-state players, but the majority of guys were from Texas, and we always wanted to represent. We see USC representing Cali. We saw Florida representing Florida. We saw LSU represent the Boot. All those teams won whenever I got into college, so it was like, well, Texas needs to come back and represent again. It was from a standpoint of representing Texas high school football as the best in the country, because our team was comprised up of so many Texas kids."

Whittaker played in seven games while dealing with a persistent knee injury. When he did get into the game, he flashed the type of quickness and big-play ability the offense sorely needed as they worked to replace Charles. After facing a gauntlet that included top 15–ranked teams Oklahoma, Missouri, and Oklahoma State, in consecutive weeks, the Longhorns would face top 10–ranked Texas Tech in Lubbock. As they headed into that game, confidence was at an all-time high following three straight wins with strong performances.

"Our confidence was already high," Whittaker said. "It was like we gained more, but we already expected to beat those teams like that. This was a team that had already had players that won a national championship. They knew exactly what it took to win the conference.

They knew exactly what it took to win a national championship, and we still had some of those players on the team. Having that type of mindset where guys knew what it took, had been there before, and knew exactly the positions that we needed to be in, that was really the confidence that allowed us to be able to feel like we deserve to be on top and the confidence to say, 'This is our conference.' We thought we were going to represent the Big 12 and we were going to be in the national championship game. Obviously the Tech game didn't go the way that we wanted it to go, but our confidence was already high before we even played Oklahoma."

The streak would end on Halloween in Lubbock when a last-second pass to Michael Crabtree helped the Red Raiders upset the Longhorns. The Longhorns sat in a three-way tie with Oklahoma and Texas Tech, and, despite holding the head-to-head win over Oklahoma, the Big 12 rules dictated that final BCS ranking would decide a three-way tie in the conference. After finishing the season unbeaten, Oklahoma got the nod from the BCS computers, leaving a disappointed Texas team for the Fiesta Bowl. At that time in college football, "style points" could play a big factor in rankings, as teams were encouraged to run the score up in order to show a more impressive résumé. While that wasn't Brown's style, the Sooners would continue to attack offensively. There was quite a bit of frustration from the team following a year when they felt they could win it all.

"I mean, we were extremely frustrated," Whittaker said. "The thing about it was Coach Brown—the way he liked to win in games was once we got up, he put in the reserves. He would run the ball, and we would chew up clock and get the game over with. What we saw from our counterparts across the Red River was Bob Stoops wanted to score. He put up points. He would leave the starters until five minutes left in the fourth quarter when they were already up by like four touchdowns. He still wanted those style points, which ultimately netted him the desired goal of playing in the national championship. Whereas if we really wanted to, Coach Brown could have had us putting up 60 points each game. So the frustration really lied there in us. We felt like they didn't take into consideration that we didn't play our starters all the way through the fourth quarter. Oklahoma did, and we beat Oklahoma doing what they were trying to do. We were frustrated, but at the end of the day we couldn't let that frustration basically sit too long, because we knew we had Beanie Wells and Ohio State coming in. They had a stacked group right there, so we knew we couldn't take them for granted. And if we wanted to prove that we were truly supposed to be in the national championship game, then we had to win that Fiesta Bowl game."

Texas did win the Fiesta Bowl following a late drive and touchdown pass to Quan Cosby. They also had to watch Oklahoma lose in the BCS National Championship Game to Florida. It's easy to envision a group of Texas players sitting around watching that game and talking about how they could have won it all. While it may not have played out that way exactly, Whittaker and the team felt they were a better matchup for Urban Meyer's Gators.

"I feel like we say that every year," Whittaker said. "Any game we lost we felt like we should have beat them. Ultimately—and I'm not going to lie, that Florida team was loaded and stacked as well—I think it would have been a really good game had we played them and not Oklahoma. Their game was good too. We just felt like we probably could have matched up against Florida a little bit better. Our defense, I felt like, was better than Oklahoma's defense, and they could have played better. So I think everybody at some point in time on our team was like, 'Yeah, we could have beat that Florida team.' I will say we had our hands full with Ohio State too. I wouldn't say it was just a given that we would go in there and win. Obviously you've got to play the game because that ultimately decides who's who, but that Florida team was really good."

The Longhorns finished the season ranked third after beating Ohio State. With multiple starters returning for 2009, there was no over-looking Texas—2008 felt like the prelude to something special, much like 2004 was the prelude to the national title. Going into off-season workouts the goal was clear, and everyone bought in.

"Everybody was all the way in for that," Whittaker said. "You had a guy like Colt, who I thought was going to come out or should have came out, and had better draft capital, in my opinion, his junior year. He was turning it down and saying, 'I'm foregoing getting drafted in at least, at the latest, third round.' He was going to be a probably first- or second-round pick, I believe, if he would have left his junior year. You had him foregoing this guaranteed money to come back for another season to try to win a national championship with Texas. That was really all the ignition that we needed. That was the spark that lit the flame for everybody to believe, 'Okay, this is our year. I know we say it every year, but we're coming back. We definitely have an opportunity.'"

Whittaker dealt with knee injuries throughout his college career. An MCL sprain during his freshman year and an LCL sprain his soph-omore year saw him miss several games. Whittaker sat out the first three contests of 2009 but came back to try and help the Texas offense add some punch. While things were clicking defensively, the offense just wasn't as dynamic as it had been in 2008. Texas was winning games, but it looked much more difficult on a week-to-week basis.

Texas desperately needed an option in the backfield to help take the running load off of McCoy.

"We didn't have a true feature back in 2009," Whittaker said. "I felt like, you know, we were trying to find an identity outside of Colt to help in the run game. Our run game was not as dominant as it was in 2008 or even in 2007. We just had a better balance offensively running the ball and throwing the ball in 2008 versus in '09. We had to shoulder, or really Colt had to shoulder a little more of the rushing attack. That also came with us not having a feature back in us doing a running back by committee. I mean it seemed like everybody got to start that season. Vondrell [McGee], myself, Tre' Newton, Cody Johnson—like we were just all rotating and trying to figure out who could be that, that every-down back. Nobody ended up surfacing that way, but the plays weren't called necessarily for it to. I guess [it could] happen that way too."

Despite troubles rushing the ball, Texas made it back to Pasadena for another shot at the national title inside the Rose Bowl. The opponent would be Nick Saban's Alabama program. The Crimson Tide were on a rise of their own, but they hadn't yet become the dynasty they are today. A win over Texas propelled Alabama into the next decade where they would win four more and take the throne as college football's premier program. That ascension would probably still have happened if they lost to Texas, but the outcome of that game will be debated forever. Alabama's strong downhill rushing attack and defense were on display against the Texas spread and a pretty strong defense in its own right. Maybe Texas would have been too much offensively if McCoy had played the entire game. The Longhorns received the opening kickoff and marched right down the field, picking up big chunks against Alabama. McCoy was hit by Alabama defensive lineman Marcell Dareus on a quarterback sneak. What looked like an ordinary hit caused McCoy to suffer a severe shoulder injury and lose feeling in his arm. The Texas program hasn't been the same since that moment, but nobody could have known that then. With McCoy out, true freshman quarterback Garrett Gilbert entered the game and played well despite some young mistakes.

"We were looking like, 'Man, is he coming back?'" Whittaker said of McCoy. "'Is he going to be okay?' In the mindset of most people on the sidelines it was like, 'Colt's coming back—that's just who he is. He's been banged up before. It hasn't fazed him. He's Colt. He's going to come through and be fine.' As the game progressed, it was like, 'Okay, Colt may not be coming back. Well, G-2 [as the players called Gilbert], you're going to have to step it up.' G-2 had performed just fine whenever he got opportunities, but it was always at the end of games, so it wasn't as if it was the same stakes. It also wasn't as if he was going against the same amount of talent that he saw against Alabama, but I do believe the belief was still there. We had a ton of talented guys that were around him that could still make plays. Obviously Jordan Shipley played a huge factor, especially in the second half and keeping us within striking distance against Alabama. There was an adjustment period that we had to make with Garrett coming in and Colt being out. The play calling changed dramatically. The way that the defense probably perceived our offense changed dramatically, and then just being able to effectively run the plays in the same type of demeanor. You know, it wasn't the same atmosphere. I mean, how could you have the same atmosphere with the redshirt senior versus a true freshman? You'll never be able to replicate that same type of demeanor and ownership of the offense. One thing that Garrett had was that we all believed in him. He was a true competitor. He was not going to back down from that moment or shy away from that moment. And that's what truly made me appreciate Garrett so much, was just the fact that he stepped right in. Coaches decided to put him in over Sherrod Harris and over John Chiles as a true freshman, and just let them go. Like they said, 'You know, this is your offense now. This is your opportunity. We get an early glimpse of what it'll be like next year. Let's go ahead and get you going and see what you got.' And so he obviously got a ton of valuable experience in that game. We all believed that he could do it."

Nobody could have foreseen what would come next. Gilbert had survived his baptism by fire and entered 2010 as the undisputed starter at quarterback. Though Texas would have to replace some pieces, the hope was that they could start building toward another run at winning it all. What happened instead was disaster. For the first time in Brown's tenure at Texas, the Longhorns had a losing season and finished at 5–7. Gilbert struggled and would transfer following the season. Gilbert wasn't the only reason for the failure—Whittaker felt the offense as a whole failed a program that returned a strong defense.

"We didn't do what we were supposed to do," Whittaker said. "That's where I put a ton of blame on the offense. I'm a part of that blame being one of the running backs out there. We just did not have that same type of intensity that the defense had. I mean, we still had like a top-15 defense in the country. But we turned the ball over so much offensively, and we did not have a consistent and reliable run game. That made it tough for Garrett to create plays. Obviously he suffered the injury too, so having an injury limited his throwing mechanics and how far we could throw downfield. So with the combination of the injury to his shoulder, the combination of us not being able to run as efficiently as we needed to own first and second down, that really limited what we were able to do. It put the defense in a bad situation because they were having to come off the field and then four or five plays later, they're right back on the field, so they didn't get enough rest in between drives. I think, ultimately, it's just the injuries mounted up along with the turnovers. We had too many turnovers, whether it was fumbles, interceptions, but offensively I think the downfall of that season was how many turnovers that we had committed as an offensive unit."

Whittaker's senior year saw the team bounce back from a losing season, and he was starting to have the type of breakout performance fans and coaches were hoping for. Averaging 5.8 yards per carry with six touchdowns midway through the season, the injury bug got Whittaker again. In a game against Missouri on the road, Whittaker tore his ACL, effectively ending his college career. The turf at Missouri's Memorial Stadium was an issue for several players, and it got to Whittaker as well. With his college career over, Whittaker would look toward the NFL, but how would a guy who played so infrequently and battled numerous injury issues be able to make it? Whittaker decided to put the work in and put his trust in God.

"Originally going into the draft after trying to rehab and recover for good—I had surgery in January because I had the injury in November or December," Whittaker said. "I had this injury in December, early December, and then I had surgery in January. It was just trying to recover as much as I could to make it in time for the Combine. Obviously I wasn't going to be able to compete or do anything from an on-field testing standpoint, but I wanted to hopefully show that I was healing up in a good manner so that they can have some positive feelings about me. Same way with the Combine recheck whenever they did it a month later, and then same thing for pro day. It was just showing that my healing was going well, and my agent is telling me, you know, I still had a great season. Obviously I wasn't able to finish everything how I wanted to finish, but I had a guy even give me as high as a third-round draft pick grade all the way to a free agency ranking. I had a huge variable window of where I was slated from a standpoint of, you know, where I could get drafted. I would have been playing in the Senior Bowl, so that would have been another opportunity to be able to showcase my abilities. So not having those things definitely hurt me. Then the draft came around, and I didn't get drafted. One of the reasons was because I still wasn't healthy and wouldn't be able to contribute to an NFL team in a timely manner or fashion. Obviously a team's not going to spend money without getting something in return. So it took me a couple of weeks after the draft happened to kind of get over that, because I didn't get a free agent deal either within those couple of weeks. So my agent was telling me, 'You know, just keep staying patient, keep working, keep working on the swelling. One of these free agent deals is going to pop up.' At that time it never popped up or manifested itself. So I was down on myself for the first couple of weeks after the draft because I didn't get drafted. I didn't get a priority free agent deal. I didn't get a free agent deal at all. It took me a couple of weeks to continue to shake off that feeling, get my confidence back, and continue to go to work. And afterward, man, I just remember myself saying, 'I'm going to give myself the best opportunity so whenever I do have a tryout or an opportunity, if that even ever comes, I want to put my best foot forward.' That opportunity came all the way in December. So I basically had to work out and train and rehab throughout that entire time, from March all the way to May—actually from February, because that's whenever the Combine was. So from February, March, April, May, and then all the way into December, you know, I'm just feeding off of everything that hasn't gone right. I'm not letting it affect me to the point where, you know, I lose sight of my ultimate goal, which was hopefully getting a tryout for an NFL team and then making the team."

Whittaker's opportunity would come after that December tryout. The Arizona Cardinals offered him a chance to make their practice squad and work his way up. Whittaker took that and ran with it, staying in the NFL for seven years with the Cardinals, Chargers, Browns, and Panthers.

"That dream became a reality whenever Arizona reached out to me and offered me a practice squad spot after I did a workout for them," Whittaker said. "Even then, you know, I did the workout, went back home, and then it wasn't until a week later after that workout that they flew me out there and signed me. I saw my first NFL contract. So that was a process and a journey in and of itself that I never take lightly because I've had football snatched away from me with that knee injury and then just understanding all the amount of work that it took. Having to get a job in the summer, having to get a job in the fall to make sure I can make ends meet while I'm still trying to train and rehab to prepare for any opportunity that may come up in a training camp situation or in the season situation. I had to be mentally strong, and I had to have a strong support group around me, which included my mother, my now-wife who was my girlfriend at the time, my brothers, my uncle—Coach Rucker was still pivotal in that. Coach Applewhite, who was my running back coach after Coach Rucker. Coach Brown was very helpful as well. Also the trainers at Texas, whether it be Bennie Wylie or Caesar Martinez or the other staff. They were the ones in there with me through the entire rehab process, working closely with me every day. That's the reason why I'm able to have played seven years in the NFL, because they believed that I could get there and helped continue to push that belief into me even after times where I didn't get drafted or didn't get a free agent deal. So that was a ton of help and support that I needed. That got me to where I am now."

Whittaker always had a heart for giving back to others. As a college student, Whittaker was heavily involved in charities, spending time at Dell Children's Medical Center visiting with sick children and spearheading other projects for the Texas football community service program. His heart came from his faith and his mother, who made sure that from a young age he understood that helping others was an important part of life.

"That was my mom," Whittaker said. "That was all my mom right there. [Growing up,] at my church that we went to on Sundays, we would go feed the homeless people. Then in the wintertime, especially getting close to Christmas, we would go and pass out blankets. My mom and some of the church members would cook huge pots of chili, and we would go out there and give blankets and chili and rice and crackers out to the homeless people right underneath the bridge at [Route] 59 in downtown Houston, right in front of Fiesta [Mart]. We would go there every single year underneath the bridge and just hand out clothes and blankets and food and just do that every single year. I never really understood why my mom made us do that, because initially she made us do it. It was just something that felt like a chore. As a kid it was like, 'Oh, I've got to do this. Here we go again. I've got to do this.' And so as I got older, once I started getting into probably about middle school, I started realizing that I *get* to do this versus I *got* to do this. I get to do this because I'm in a position to be able to do that. That started kicking in. Once I got into high school, it took it to a whole other level with how much people are influenced by sports. At the time football was everything, and if you were a star player in my city, you were basically a professional athlete in their eyes. So having that type of mantra or label on you meant a lot. So I wanted my time, whenever people saw me, I wanted them to say, 'He's a, he's a great athlete on the field, but he's an even better person off the field.' That was kind of my mindset that my mom created within my lifestyle without me even really knowing it. That continued to foster and grow into me wanting to be known as a selfless person. I never wanted to be called selfish. I want to be able to say that I was selfless. So that was something that has always stuck with me since I was at a young age.

"Even to this day that's why I started my nonprofit organization with my mom and my wife. That's why I still give back to the community today. Just today I was a part of an interview panel for Vista Ridge High School for all of the autistic and special-needs kids just talking to people and giving them opportunities to express themselves as well. And then just if I have a way to give, and this is from a biblical aspect, which is where I was raised up in the church, and the Christian belief is those who give, they feel much better. It's better to give than it is to receive. So that's something I've taken to heart. If have it, I will give it. I don't mind because I know there is somebody that needs it more than me. At the same time I get more satisfaction or as much satisfaction from that than what somebody may get from the actual thing that may be given away. Just that feeling is all that I need to be able to carry on. So that's what truly drives my spirit and something that my mother instilled in me at an early age that I had no idea she was doing that until, you know, I started getting a deeper appreciation of life and kind of the opportunities that were given to me just because of who I was born into, the family I was born into, and the opportunities that my mother gave me and the sacrifices made from so many people to get me to where I'm at."

Whittaker finished his NFL career and returned to Austin, where he became involved in a few different ventures. His nonprofit foundation Fozzy's Future Heroes is an organization that aims to support the development of youth in areas of athletics and education through several different events. Whittaker also became involved in the media side of the business, landing a gig with ESPN's Longhorn Network and a radio show on SiriusXM.

"Longhorn Network started my senior year actually," Whittaker said. "That was the first year LHN came into town. Obviously they wanted to create a positive relationship with the school and the athletes that would be on the network a lot. It really showed an opportunity for me to go into a field that I think I would have truly enjoyed. Originally I wanted to go into football operations and be like the guy, George Wynn who I talked about, who helped recruit me to Texas. I wanted to be that person for UT or another college, because of the influence and the impact that he had just trying to make sure that these students and college athletes [know] the opportunities that are available for them. Going to a full-ride university like The University of Texas, you can get your education even if you never play a down of football. You know, just don't get in trouble—don't get kicked out. That was basically one of the things that I wanted to be a part of and help people just transition from high school to college and help them understand you can be a great football player, but I want you to be better people as well. That was my initial goal. I started realizing that I didn't necessarily want to work those same type of football hours once I was done playing football. So I was like, 'Maybe I could go into the broadcasting route. My undergrad degree was in communications.

Maybe I can go that route.' I thought it would be great. A lot of people always had told me up to that point that I speak very well in public. Whenever I would do interviews people said, 'You know, it sounded great.' So I was like, 'Okay, maybe I can maybe turn that into a profession and still cover the game that I truly love.' I got with Ande Wall—she's the executive producer over at Longhorn Network. I got with her back in 2011 during the first year, and it was just like, 'Hey, Ande, I am interested in what you guys do. I just want to come around. I just want to see how everything works. If you would have me, I would love to be on your show [as] a guest. Just an appearance, or to help interview people, whatever the case may be. I just want to be around. If opportunities arise, please don't hesitate in texting me or emailing me, and I'll find a way to make it work.' Ande took those words to heart, and every single off-season she would reach out to me, and I would come on a show or during the bye week—I will come onto the show and do a segment with Ricky or V.Y. or whoever the case may be. That ended up progressing into me actually helping host, you know, pro days with Lowell Galindo. So me and Lowell would do pro days with the Emmanuel Acho, and then we would just talk about each athlete as they are going through their testing. That obviously led to me being on *Texas GameDay* before the game. We would do the two-hour pregame show. I started off with one show and then moved up to six shows. Now for the past two seasons I've been on there full time. That turned into something where Ande saw something within me. She also gave me the opportunity, and then she also followed up on that ask by me. I wanted to be truly transparent that I wanted to be a part of Longhorn Network while it was here, and she was like, 'Okay, we're going to give you opportunities.' That was truly amazing and a dream come true. I love the broadcasting aspect of it. It keeps me still involved with the school, and it also keeps me involved with football in general. I get to go more in depth in an analysis on how I'm breaking down film, on breaking down play calling in it. It gives me that kind of same adrenaline rush as if I'm preparing for a football game that I'm about to play in. I loved it from that aspect. Ever since then Ande and I have had a great relationship, and we continue to have a great relationship. So she's always looked out for me since 2011. Back in 2016 I talked to a guy while I was in Carolina named Michael Mazvinsky, who is over [at] SiriusXM—channel 375, which is the Big 12 Network. Last year was my first year actually doing the radio broadcast. I had never done the radio broadcast side of things. I've always just done the televised stuff with Longhorn Network or interviews with local TV stations. Maz, who is a Texas graduate as well, came up [and] said, 'Hey, I want to have you on the show. You're going to be partnered up with Ari Temkin, who's been on the show for a couple of years already. It's only since 2018 that the Big 12 Network channel was actually introduced to SiriusXM. He's been here a couple of years, but he's going to be your cohost, and you're going to go every Monday morning. You got three hours, and you're going to talk about football and talk about all the Big 12 sports.' So I did that last year, and this is year number two that I've been doing that. That's been really cool from the aspect of switching it up and how the variance between radio broadcast versus TV broadcast differs. It's just the different type of conversations you're able to have and the approach to the preparation for the shows."

Whittaker is also venturing into the business world. He and his business partners began preparations to open a gym in 2020. The COVID-19 pandemic created several obstacles for the business, but they were finally able to open in early 2022. Whittaker made his impact on the field, but his impact off of it has been far greater. Whittaker and his brothers were the first in his family to graduate from college, and he's looking to continue that legacy and create a path for others.

"This has been about two years in the making," Whittaker said. "Since 2020, right before the pandemic started, my wife and I—along with our two business partners, Eric and Nikki—we opened up a gym. It's a franchise gym called Burn Boot Camp, and it's right in Cedar Park.... It has been truly amazing. With COVID happening, it pushed us back by a few months because of the shortages and the price of lumber and everything that everybody else is going through. We finally got open in January, and it gave us [the] opportunity to start putting our vision into play and not just have everything written down in words. So having the gym open for our fourth week has been truly amazing. It's been going very well so far. We want to continue to keep that traction and momentum that we've created up to this point to continue to springboard us to have a successful first year. I've learned so much being an entrepreneur so far and the owner, from the aspect of finding the lease, the real estate that we need to be able to get our gym built, what certifications and permits we need to have in place so that we can go on to the next step. Then the architectural plans that's put in place, and then the engineering that's put in place, the plumbing, the amount of detail that's put into our brand. Everything from what our reception area looks like, what our workout area looks like, our childcare area. So all of that has been truly eye-opening from an entrepreneurial standpoint. Then hiring staff. That's been another issue that's been ongoing with COVID. It's been truly amazing to be able to be in a position to know what it takes to be an owner and start actually having the access to break the cycle. My mom, she didn't have a four-year degree. She didn't graduate college. I was the third one to graduate college. Both my brothers graduated college, and so I'm following in their footsteps graduating college, and then I'm the first one to own a business and be an actual business owner. I'm trying to teach not only just my kids the ways that you can navigate this world to hopefully be successful but also other people that may have looked up to me or other people that are interested in some of the same developments that I've been trying to get into. I want to share that knowledge that I've gained with whoever is willing to listen to me. It's a lot that goes into planning and preparing for a business, and being able to share just maybe one or two nuances that they're able to take away with it would have been worth it for a conversation. People poured that information into me to help us get to where we are now."

CHAPTER 6

Roy Miller

Fort Hood is the one of the most populous military bases in the world. Nestled in the central Texas city of Killeen, located halfway between Waco and Austin, the base sits on over 150,000 acres and is a city unto itself. As one of the premier training bases in the world, it brings new blood to Texas often as families transfer in. Roy Miller was part of one of those families. The former Longhorn defensive tackle has a storied career in Austin and went on to a long and productive career in the NFL.

Miller was an anchor on the Texas defensive line that won a Fiesta Bowl and played for a national title. When Miller arrived in Killeen he was a relative unknown. A short and squatty defensive tackle, Miller played football sporadically before a growth spurt turned him into a lean and mean force on the defensive line. Following a summer away from Killeen, coaches at the newly formed Shoemaker High School got a look at Miller and made sure he did what was necessary to be part of the program. Though they didn't know exactly what they had, Miller showed his stuff quickly.

"My dad was in the army," Miller said, "so we got to Killeen. We were moving around a lot. Military families, they go visit when the summertime comes. They just take off and go visit other family, so I ended up coming late to Shoemaker. By that time I kind of hit a growth spurt—I was about 6'2" coming from middle school. I think I was a good player, but I was just kind of shorter. I was probably about 5'7" or 5'6". Once I hit that growth spurt, I didn't even realize it. People would tell me, but I guess I just wasn't used to being that much taller. But I get to Shoemaker High School, and coaches were on me to get my physical and get into football. I just noticed that I was so much bigger than a lot of other players. So they started me off on a freshman B team because I hadn't played in a while. I'm getting like seven or eight sacks a quarter, and they just took me out of the game. From that point they moved me up. They didn't believe in starting freshmen or putting freshmen on varsity. At that point in time I felt like something had changed. I felt like, you know, I've been lifting weights and stuff throughout the summers up until then, but at that point, I just, I felt like I could be good at it. I didn't know how good, but I just felt like I could be good."

Miller spent the early years of his life in Virginia, where his father was originally stationed. Deep in ACC country, Miller was a world away from the burnt orange and tradition of The University of Texas. At that time the North Carolina Tar Heels was the program Miller had his eye on. UNC was a rising program under Miller's future head coach Mack Brown, and their iconic "Carolina Blue" color scheme was everywhere in the late '90s. When Miller arrived in Killeen he gained a new appreciation for the influence the Longhorns had in the state of Texas.

"When I lived in Virginia I wanted to play for the Tar Heels," Miller said. "They were just a good team all around. Mack Brown was there, but I didn't know that at the time. But, you know, my family didn't necessarily go to college, so we didn't have like a college team or anything like that. When I got to Texas, you start driving around, and you start seeing all those Longhorns on the back [of] everybody's bumpers. You start seeing that orange everywhere, and you know it's a different place. Everybody's representing, and I think that's why so many people become fans of the university—because of the dominance across the world. Especially Texas."

Central Texas has always been a largely under-recruited area. While most colleges focus on the talent centers in the state, including Dallas–Fort Worth, greater Houston, and East Texas, the Hill Country area wasn't mined nearly as much. The region didn't lack talent, producing names including Derrick Johnson, Quan Cosby, and Tommie Harris. Harris would have a massive impact on Miller's life and career, but that would come later down the road. Early on, Miller knew he would have to get out and sell himself in order to be recruited. Miller came about at a time before social media and companies such as Hudl, which hosts player film online for anyone to see and makes the talent discovery aspect of recruiting much easier. If prospects wanted college coaches to know who they were, they would have to send their film out in DVD reels for coaches to watch. After Miller began to play well at the varsity level, he decided to get out on the road and shop his tape around. He found what he thought would be his future home just 30 minutes north, at Baylor.

"Being at Shoemaker High School, I want to say it was two or three years old when I got there," Miller said. "The last person that came out of that area was Tommie Harris. Obviously he was a really good player, but the area, for whatever reason, wasn't really heavily recruited. I don't remember seeing a lot of college coaches and stuff like that coming through. For me, I'd seen some of the seniors get letters and stuff like that. I didn't see all that stuff. I had to start pretty much pumping myself. I had to send out video. Initially I took a trip. One of my first places where I got my first scholarship was at Baylor. I told my dad at the time, 'We should go take a trip and get some [of] this video out. Let's just go pretty much knock on the doors of these coaches and show them our film and see what they say.' Baylor was 30 or 40 minutes up the road. That was our first stop. I go in there and I give them my tape. They just kind of told me thank you, because they get tape all the time. They go in the back and check it out, and I see Guy Morriss and the staff—it's just a different energy. The coaches come out and are looking at us and asking about if we want a tour around the campus. I didn't think any of this was possible. In my mind, I was thinking about this player at UNT [University of North Texas] named Booger [Brandon] Kennedy. He was a shorter defensive tackle. During that time everyone was looking for giant defensive tackles like Frank Okam and Rod Wright and all of those kinds of guys. I thought I needed to go to UNT and places like that who utilized shorter defensive tackles to push my film around. Baylor came out and offered me a scholarship and took us around campus."

Once Baylor offered, Miller was ready to make his commitment. He was going to be a sophomore soon, but he thought the Bears would be a perfect situation for him. It was then that Miller learned the meaning of an "uncommittable offer." In recruiting, offers are verbal agreements that the school will extend a scholarship. Just like a player's commitment is a verbal agreement to accept the offer, both are nonbinding. Many times, schools will extend offers to begin a recruitment, but they might not be prepared to accept a commitment at that time. When Miller informed the coaches of his desire to be a Bear, he was shocked to learn they wouldn't take him.

"I was immediately like, 'I want to commit,'" Miller said. "I told Coach that we wanted to commit, and we didn't think this was even possible. Coach Morriss told me he couldn't accept it at the moment. We were just shocked because they just offered me a scholarship. He told me there would be a lot of people that would offer me a scholarship, and I just needed to take my time. He told us that, and I'll just never forget being shocked from that experience. That was the first major university to offer me."

Miller was new to recruiting, and his first lesson in how the game is played on that end shocked him. Perhaps Morriss was doing him a favor by letting him know that he would go on to pick up many more offers, but as a young man he wasn't sure how to handle it.

"At 15 years old I didn't know how to take it," Miller said. "The way I was raised, it was to be loyal to whoever believes in you. I was ready, and I was just honored by it. Living 30 or 40 minutes away, I thought it was perfect. It was right at home. I had no idea I'd have a shot at Texas or any of the other schools, so I didn't know how to take it at that time. I wasn't upset, but I think I was just disappointed."

Tommie Harris loomed large in Killeen. Coming out of Killeen Ellison High School in 2001, Harris chose Oklahoma over Texas and went on to a star-studded career. He remained active in the Killeen community, returning often to mentor younger players from the area. He connected with Miller early on, and Miller would often travel with Harris' parents to Oklahoma games to watch him play. Though he didn't generate interest from the Sooners early on, Miller would eventually find his way onto Bob Stoops' radar. At that time, recruits would receive letters letting them know that schools were interested, but most of the time the communication just served as a way to keep relationships warm without engaging full force in the recruitment. For players such as Miller, letters would pile up in their mailboxes every day and most of them were generic in nature. One of those letters arrived from Oklahoma one day, but the content was anything but generic.

"I committed to Oklahoma my sophomore year in high school," Miller said. "Darrell Wyatt was at Oklahoma at the time, and his sister was a teacher in one of the Killeen schools. At that time Oklahoma was rolling. They had won a national championship a couple of years before. I was a fan of a lot of those guys like Jason White and the defense they had with guys like Dan Cody and Teddy Lehman and all those guys. I was a fan of that team, and I got a letter. I started to get a little more momentum as far as recruiting. I want to say Oklahoma just sent me a letter. It didn't seem like anything special because we would get stacks of mail. I just kind of opened it up not expecting anything, and it said I'd been offered, and Bob Stoops signed it. I always wanted to be like Tommie Harris. I grew up in Killeen admiring what he was doing. He became a mentor to me, so as soon as that happened I felt like it was a way to honor the relationship that we built and just try to follow in his footsteps."

Miller made his commitment to Oklahoma and thought his recruitment was over. As Miller prepared for life as a future Sooner, his relationship with the staff ate at him. Sure he had an offer and a good relationship with the assistants recruiting him, but Miller never found the family feel he was looking for at Oklahoma. During the spring of his junior year, Miller made the decision to decommit from Oklahoma to reevaluate his options. Oklahoma could have saved the commitment, but Miller felt disrespected by the staff in the way they handled it.

"At that time Oklahoma was rolling," Miller said. "They were No. 1 or No. 2 or whatever. They were highly ranked every year. I'd go up to the school, and, for whatever reason, I never met the whole coaching staff. A lot of other places I went to, they were happy to introduce me to all of these different people. It just felt like I only knew the position coach and my area recruiter. It didn't really feel like a family. I'd go up to some of the games and some of the events, and I felt like they were spending a lot of time bringing other recruits and other people and praising them. I felt like I was watching recruiting happening for everyone else going there, and it didn't feel good to me. When I started feeling like that, I was just like, 'Let me go see some of these other schools, and let me go see what Texas is about.'

"I ended up going to a junior day at Texas. I got spotted, and people wrote articles and stuff about it. I remember [Oklahoma defensive coordinator] Coach Bobby Jack Wright called me and said they saw I was at Texas. He asked if I was committed and where my head was at. He told me, 'We're going to win with or without you, so you need to make your mind up.' I was just like, 'I guess you don't need me.' I decommitted that day. I pulled over on the side of the road, and it was the toughest decision I had to make as a young person. You get close to fans who are in your community and all of these schools we played against. We wore hats. My whole family had all kinds of Oklahoma stuff. So I pulled over on the side of the road, and I was just very nervous. I told him that if they were going to win with or without me, I was going to take my commitment back. I hung up the phone and went about what I was doing.

"They called me all day and all night. The next day Coach Wright was sitting in my coach's office. He had all of his championship rings on his hand and had his feet kicked up on my coach's desk. I just felt like that was kind of disrespectful. I felt disrespected already, but when I saw his feet up on the desk, I felt like that was just another sign that it wasn't supposed to happen. I pretty much told him again that I was opening this thing back up."

Once he was back on the market, Miller started to look into other schools. He visited Utah, where his cousin played under Urban Meyer. His parents were set to make a move to Washington, so Miller started to fix his eyes on the West Coast. UCLA received a visit and LSU continued to push. The Tigers might have been able to land Miller, but they continued to insist he come to summer camp. The door was still open for Oklahoma, but the relationship had sustained a fair amount of damage. Outside of his Junior Day visit to Austin he hadn't received much interest from the Longhorns. Miller previously built a good relationship with Texas defensive coordinator Greg Robinson, but the Longhorns weren't seriously engaged. Robinson ended up leaving Austin after Miller's junior season and a lapse in contact dropped Texas from the picture.

"There was a coaching change, and Greg Robinson came in," Miller said. "It was his first year at Texas, so he kind of hit the recruiting trail late. By this time they were telling me that they were sorry because they came to me my junior year. I was kind of offended. I think like a lot of players do, such as the Baker Mayfields and those guys. They are so close, and then they don't get a scholarship, and they spend the rest of their career hating Texas. I was the opposite. I just loved that burnt orange. There was something in me always drawing me toward Austin. I was on an Oklahoma official visit one time, and I was sitting there as they were getting ready to play somebody at night. We were watching Texas play Kansas, and it was that fourth-down play where V.Y. has the ball. I was like, 'Man, how cool would it be to play on a team with a guy like that?' So Greg Robinson came in and was telling me about trying to catch up. I was talking to him about Derrick Johnson.

[Johnson] had just won the Nagurski Award, and he was telling me how Derrick was complaining about the gym at the hotel because he couldn't get over 10 miles per hour on the treadmill. He started recruiting me late, and we had a whole lot of conversations about ball. He'd call me after games and stuff like that. He ended up leaving and there was kind of this gap of silence when I didn't talk to anybody."

Robinson was replaced by Gene Chizik as defensive coordinator at Texas. After picking up the slack from the loss of communication, Chizik began to pursue Miller. The Longhorns still hadn't offered, but they asked him to come to a camp in the summer. Harris would once again become a part of Miller's recruitment as he helped pay for Miller to attend the event. Miller was offered during the camp, and the Longhorns were officially in the game.

"Coach Robinson told me he was leaving," Miller said. "Chizik came in, and all of a sudden Texas asks me to come out to a football camp in the summer. It's an interesting story because Tommie Harris helped pay for me to go to the Texas camp. At that time I probably shouldn't have said anything about it, but I told them, and Tommie got kind of upset with me. There's no reason for me to go to a Texas camp if Oklahoma is where he's at and where he supports. I go to the camp and go through all the drills, and Coach Brown calls me in and tells me they are going to offer me a scholarship. Tommie was upset I told some people. I couldn't imagine me helping a child go to an Oklahoma football camp now and they tell everyone. The thing about Tommie is he's just been a supporter for me over the years. Even with my decision to go to Texas, he just told me to do what's best for me and always supported that."

Chizik took over the recruitment. Miller always felt drawn to Austin, and that year he attended the Red River Shootout to see Texas face Oklahoma. As he spent more time at Texas he found the family vibe he was looking for. Fostering that atmosphere was huge for Brown in recruiting, and, once again, his wife, Sally Brown, made an impact.

"I went to the OU game two years prior, so I knew that these two places were the real deal," Miller said. "I went to games in Austin, and I got to hang out with everyone. Going to Texas just felt like family. Mack Brown is big on the family atmosphere. Miss Sally is part of that family with him. It just felt good to have all the coaches welcome me and make me feel at home. It just felt like being in Austin as a kid with all the things to do—it was like why would I go...anywhere else when Austin is right here?"

The Red River Shootout is as unique of an experience as there is in college sports. As a recruit, Miller got an up-close look at the environment on two separate occasions. He attended the game as an OU commit previously, and he went back to Dallas in his senior year as a Texas recruit to see it from their side.

"Everything about it was exciting," Miller said. "Everything was just black and white. There's the other guys and there's this. You walk through the fair and you hear chanting from both sides. There is this competitive, intriguing feeling being on one side or the other. There's the State Fair [of Texas] and all the food. It's an experience. As you get close to that thing, there's more and more. You get inside, and the stadium is split half and half. It's intense. Being in there and hearing both sides talk so much trash to each other and just being a part of it—I feel like a lot of non-OU and -Texas fans go just to be a part of it. It was definitely a changing moment in my life. I haven't seen anything like that outside of that game."

Miller took his official visit to Texas late in December during the annual Texas football banquet weekend. Miller was hosted at Texas by All-American defensive tackle Rod Wright, and, in true big-man fashion, he vividly remembers the food on the trip. But more than anything, the family atmosphere at Texas was the overwhelming feeling that reeled him in.

"I'm a simple person," Miller said. "I remember all the good food. I remember going in the room, and they had all this candy and stuff. I was in there gorging on all that. I went to other places on official visits. Oklahoma kind of has their own version they were doing, and Adrian Peterson was my host. At Texas we'd all hang out together. All of the players were just one big group, and I just didn't feel that at any other place. More than anything I felt like I wanted to be a part of that."

Miller was set to make his commitment a few weeks later in San Antonio at the U.S. Army All-American Bowl. That announcement would be a formality as Miller left his official visit as a silent commit to the Longhorns. As he headed off to San Antonio, he started to get the feeling he would be a part of something special. Texas already held a commitment from five-star quarterback Ryan Perrilloux and was in the mix for elite prospects Fred Rouse and Martellus Bennett.

"I just remember my dad was going back and forth to Iraq," Miller said. "When he came in, we went and visited Texas, and I already knew I wanted to be a Longhorn. After showing him around, they felt good about the place. We went in Coach Brown's office, and he pulled everybody in. Right there in his office I told him we wanted to be Longhorns. We definitely committed early, and from that point forward I went to try and recruit guys at the U.S. Army game. It was interesting because at that time Ryan Perrilloux and Martellus Bennett and Fred Rouse were all guys leaning to Texas. I was sitting there thinking we were going to have a crazy class. All of these guys were basically committed. We had Jamaal Charles and Jerrell

Wilkerson, who was also a beast at running back. I didn't think there was a better class in the world—and I hate to say this, but when those guys committed elsewhere, I was like, 'Damn.' I want to say I was the highest-rated recruit, and I had a lot of comfort in these other guys being with me and what was happening at Texas. I knew there would be a lot of pressure on me to become the star. The other guys who came in with me turned out to be some great players in that class, but I was talking to everyone I could. At that time guys like Martellus and them didn't really feel like they were sold, so I was spending a lot of time trying to solidify their commitments. At that game, guys turn into showmen. You've got cameras everywhere, and I remember Martellus did like a horns-up and a horns-down picture. Guys were just doing stuff like that. I was talking to guys like DeMarcus Granger and Ndamukong Suh."

As an army brat, the chance to play in the U.S. Army All-American Bowl was a special moment for Miller. The game held annually in San Antonio honored the military and was played in front of a large group of soldiers.

"I remember when they told me I got picked, that's the first thing I thought about," Miller said. "I didn't know these things were even available, but what a way to represent my community and my dad. They had a rally when I committed to the game, and they asked my dad to speak. That made me feel good. He spoke for like 20 minutes, and everybody was all cheering. It definitely felt good. San Antonio is maybe two hours away from Killeen, so a lot of coaches and teachers were able to come out, which made it a really cool experience for me."

Miller's 2005 class was known for disappointment on signing day. After missing out on the big trio of Perrilloux, Rouse, and Bennett, Texas signed just 14 players and ranked No. 13 in the nation. Though the group wasn't big on quantity, it ended up producing quite a bit of quality. Miller enrolled at Texas alongside Colt McCoy, Jamaal Charles, Henry Melton, Jermichael Finley, Roddrick Muckelroy, Chris Hall, and several others. Miller arrived in Austin just in time for Young to lead the team to a national championship. Miller wasn't a bystander during his freshman season—despite a loaded defensive line in Austin, Miller appeared in 10 games, including the Rose Bowl.

"I come from a culture where I'm always sitting, barking at guys because we lost a lot in high school," Miller said. "When I got to Texas, these guys were doing that to me and other guys. I realized from the first day I walked into the weight room it was a different level. In fact my first day in the weight room I threw up just trying to keep up with these guys and their intensity. Rashad Bobino was probably the first person I saw when I went in there. Just the energy from him and the other guys was crazy. He was a freshman at the time, but he ended up starting. I could just tell the demand and the expectations were high. Everything that we did we did together. We sacrificed and did our voluntary workouts. Guys demanded the best out of each other, and that was definitely my first impression. If I didn't get in line, these guys were going to do something special whether I wanted to join or not."

Texas dazzled on the field in 2005 behind the elite talent of Young and a physical defense. Texas would head to Pasadena to face USC, a team tabbed by ESPN as the greatest of all time. Despite the stakes of the game, Miller never felt the pressure to win. Their preparation and focus were where they needed to be, and they always had the best player on the field in Young.

"I had a lot of mixed thoughts," Miller said. "Obviously it was great. As a team we never really felt pressure at any point of the season. We always felt that with V.Y. we always had a chance. I hate to put that much pressure on one person, but whether he was in the locker room dancing or trying to make someone laugh on the field or just extending plays on the field, we never felt like we didn't have a chance. He was a junior too, so we felt like if we didn't win it that year we would do it next year. It wasn't really about a championship—it was more about us playing at our highest level. We never felt the pressure to win. We knew what we were representing and that was the most important thing. It was all the hard work and everything. We just wanted to put that on the field, so heading into Pasadena and that championship when they were talking about David and Goliath and us playing the best football team of all time in USC, we were like, 'We've got a résumé too.' It's crazy—even when we were down against Oklahoma State or different games throughout the season like Ohio State, there was always this thought in our minds that we have a chance. You don't have that on every team, but on that team we always had that optimism, and it's rightful that it ended in a championship that year."

Winning a championship is both a blessing and a curse. Now on top of the mountain, Texas football would transition from Young's era to McCoy's. The 2006 and 2007 seasons saw growing pains as the Longhorns stumbled at times. Players, including Miller, were thrust into leadership positions, and it was up to them to establish a new culture on the roster after receiving the blueprint from the players who came before them.

"We won a championship, and that was a pain," Miller said. "Every recruit that came in and every parent that came in with that recruit started having this sense of unearned pride. We could just see that guys felt like they won the championship themselves just by committing and coming to Texas. That became an issue for the Longhorns. All of a sudden we had to come in and rein guys in. That wasn't how we did it—gloating and walking around like we'd done something. That wasn't how we were going to win. We were the class that was able to see the formula of how it was done, and we saw how those guys got to that point and cared about each other. We cared as a team. Everybody put their ego aside. People were just playing—just trying to be the best they could be for each other. I tell people Mack Brown did an excellent job selling the culture. All the stars aligned for Coach Brown. This was a time when Texas rap music was on the map. Paul Wall and all of those guys were on the scene, and Texas was cool at the time. Coach Brown had us as the best of Texas. We were a team made of Texans, and we felt like we represented something more. We represented all of Texas high school and the coaching association. It was just the way he had us carry ourselves. All of that stuff felt like it continued from high school, and I really can't stress the importance of that. The culture that the guys before us created was untouched. There were just a lot of cultural changes, and Coach Brown created this ultimate culture. He topped it off by making it a family atmosphere, and I got wrapped up in there. It created an atmosphere that we didn't want to let [each other] down. It was this rich tradition and rich history in front of us, and we felt like it was our duty to go out there and give it all we had."

Nobody expected much from Texas in 2008, but the Longhorns were primed for a big run. McCoy was entering his third season as the starter, having navigated his first two seasons and working through the growing pains of the position. Heading into 2008, the team felt they had all of the right pieces in place.

"We knew Colt was good, but it was going to be hard to step into V.Y.'s shoes," Miller said. "Obviously he's not V.Y., but in our mind we were wondering who would run around and extend plays. A lot

of people would say in '05 that V.Y. won the national championship, but we knew there were a lot of other guys who would continue
on to play, and we knew those guys were really good players. When
Colt started slinging that ball around we had that same feeling, and
everyone was in shock Colt could mature that quick. There are plenty
of guys who go out in practice and do everything, but they disap-
pear in games. Colt excelled under the lights, and we had our defense
and our squad together. We felt like we had a chance every single
year. Heading into 2008 we felt like defensively we had everything
we needed. Offensively we felt like we were in good shape too, but
defensively we felt like we could shut everybody down. We had some
really good young players that weren't even starting. We had Keenan
Robinson, Sergio Kindle, Jared Norton, Lamarr Houston, Brian
Orakpo, Henry Melton, and guys like that. We had Earl Thomas and
Aaron Williams. Going into 2008 we felt like we had to do it. This
was our last shot for the 2005 class. Me and Orakpo and a couple of
guys took that into our own hands and felt like we were going to make
it happen one way or another."

The biggest catalyst for the 2008 team was the addition of defensive coordinator Will Muschamp. A mythical hero in college football
circles, Muschamp was known for his physically dominant defenses
and his insane energy on the field. Muschamp was more than just the
character fans saw on the sidelines each week—he always operated
at a level of high intensity. Texas fans are familiar with a video from
halftime of a game in 2009 when Muschamp punched a [whiteboard]
and screamed, "Do your job." While he was a shock to the system in
Austin, Miller felt he was exactly what the team needed.

"The first time we had an off-season workout, and we barely know
him," Miller said. "We were trying to gauge the relationship and

figure out what kind of coach he was going to be. We'd all seen the videos online where he was called 'Coach Boom,' and he's teaching us this pursuit drill during the workout. He had a certain way of doing it, and we run out there as the first-team defense to run the drill, and we mess it up. He said, 'This is why you guys don't win.' He called us soft. We were taken aback. We were trying to lick our wounds from the year before and forget it, but we knew we weren't soft. We were like, 'Who is this guy calling us out?' From that point, it just never stopped. Everybody had this idea that they didn't want to let him down and hear his voice yelling. He held us to a standard. We went over the details, walked through things, and prepared so much that it was just like, 'How could we mess up?' There are millions of people watching a game, but there's only one person you'd be afraid of if you made a bad play. You did not want to go back to this meeting or film. That video of him punching the [whiteboard], that happened pretty often. He was calling guys out in every single way. A lot of guys couldn't take it. There were guys who were all of a sudden hanging out in the library instead of coming to practice. At the end of the day, he's that type of guy. He will get on you, but he will love on you and celebrate with you too. I got in a situation with him myself, but at the end of the day it's all for the common goal. He's one of my favorite coaches."

The Red River Shootout always had special meaning for Miller, having previously been committed to the Sooners. Miller went 3–1 during his career against Oklahoma, and the game itself helped to mend some fences between Miller and the staff he spurned. In his final game against the Sooners, Miller contributed three tackles and a quarterback pressure against the Sooners' vaunted offensive line. He also lined up in a goal line package at fullback where he dropped a designed pass for a would-be touchdown. Coming out of that game, the team knew their hard work was paying off.

"When I decommitted, I really felt bad for some of the people I committed to," Miller said. "I'm one of those people that I don't like to let people down. I never got to close that chapter once they began calling. By that time I'd made my mind up, and I was done. I didn't really talk to the Oklahoma coaches after that. I remember the first year in the Cotton Bowl. We go in there, and the coaches wouldn't talk to me or wouldn't even look at me. Some of the fans were talking trash to me. I was expecting that, but it was definitely a weird feeling for me because I always cared about what other people think as far as me saying what I was going to do. Eventually I became closer with some of those coaches just out of respect for the game. They were competing against us, and we were able to mend some of those relationships.

Every year we knew that the championship was going through the Cotton Bowl. That year was just a little more heightened. We knew that to make a statement, we were going to have to beat them. The good thing about those games—you didn't have to wait. You wake up at 7:00 AM and get on the bus and go right to it. You don't get a whole lot of time to think about it. That was the biggest offensive line I'd ever seen. We knew that it was going to be won up front and we had to get to Sam Bradford. To get everything we talked about all summer, we truly relied on the work we put in. We knew for all that stuff to come to fruition, it was going to happen that day. That was one of the toughest games I'd ever played in. At that time Colt was the most efficient passer in the nation, but that day he threw me a bad pass at fullback. I turned around, and I couldn't even see the ball. Those guys teased me, and I told Coach [Brown], 'Don't ever throw me that ball.

I'm having the biggest battle of my life playing defense against these giants.' That game was a confidence booster for the year. I played against so many Rimington Award nominees that year, so I was used to the high competition at center. We walked into that game, and I felt like it was one of those games where you find out your identity."

After beating Oklahoma, Texas was ranked the top team in the country. With the national spotlight on the Longhorns, Texas took the field playing three straight top-15 matchups against Missouri, Oklahoma State, and Texas Tech. Miller set the tone on the first play of the Missouri game by blowing up a reverse to Jeremy Maclin deep in the backfield as the Longhorns rolled to a big victory. After beating Oklahoma State, Texas lost in a thriller to Texas Tech in Lubbock.

"There were just so many teams every single week," Miller said. "We were playing against these top-10 teams, and there was always the question of how we were going to respond. I used to go around the locker room talking trash and telling guys how we were going to play and reminding them about the work we put in and giving them some thoughts before we took the field. I remember in different games challenging different people, and in that game I told them I was going to make a big play early. That was just one of those things about that year. We had guys who would say it and then they would actually do it. It was like being a part of a movie or something. The challenge and the guys rising to the occasion is what I'm talking about throughout those years. There were so many challenges. Obviously the Tech game didn't turn out well, but when guys were challenged, I felt we rose to the occasion. One play that year and we would have been talking about something completely different. It's still a painful memory."

After missing out on the Big 12 Championship and a chance at a BCS National Championship berth, Texas found themselves in the

Fiesta Bowl against Ohio State. In Miller's final college game, he won defensive MVP honors with three tackles, two pressures, and a sack against the Buckeyes.

"It felt good," Miller said. "I was asked to do a lot of things that year where I felt like I was taking it for the team. I was taking on double teams and trying to push the pocket instead of being able to put myself in the position to make the most plays. I didn't even know I won the MVP. I was walking around celebrating with teammates, and one of the guys in a suit came up and asked if I was Roy. He told me to come with him, and I found out then. Just to be recognized and after seeing so many guys win so many different awards while at Texas—that was definitely the icing on the cake for me."

Miller finished his career playing in 49 games and starting in 19. After being selected in the third round of the 2009 NFL Draft by the Tampa Bay Buccaneers, Miller played nine seasons of professional ball with the Bucs, Jacksonville Jaguars, and Kansas City Chiefs. A father to four children, Miller is now settled in Jacksonville where he's involved in several foundations and planning to marry his fiancée in the summer of 2022. Miller is still heavily involved in the community, volunteering for several foundations and mentoring kids regularly. He returns to Austin for a game or two each year and tries to stay connected with the program.

"I've had a couple of surgeries recently, so I'm trying to get my body back healthy," Miller said. "I've got a couple of businesses here and there. Really I'm just being a father and getting married this June. All of that keeps me busy. All the wedding planning and stuff like that keeps me busy. Before the pandemic I would go to a game or two a year. The last two years have just been a little bit different. I was actually talking to some of the coaches last summer when I was getting ready to help coach one of the summer camps. They welcome us back in. I normally go back for at least a game or two, and I will this coming season."

Miller's recruitment took several twists and turns on a road that would eventually lead him to Austin. Though it was stressful at times, Miller has nothing but gratitude for the experience. His one regret would come back to face him as he prepared to enter the NFL. Though he always tried to show respect to coaches, an interaction he had with UCLA defensive line coach Don Johnson during his recruitment reminded him that he could have shown more gratitude.

"I'm grateful for everything that happened," Miller said. "I'm thankful for every single scholarship and every relationship that I made. I was sitting at the NFL Combine, and I see this coach from UCLA. He had come to my house, but I was sold on Texas already. He was trying to make his last pitch to me, and I was working out or doing something, so I took my time to get back home. I get home, and he's talking to my parents. He flew in from California, so I'm sure he was feeling a certain way having to wait so long to talk to me. I sit in there, and I'm talking to him, and we have a conversation. I wasn't too excited to talk to him. I had a Texas bracelet on and I'm sure he saw that. I don't feel like that was the most respectful thing I could do, so I always felt bad about that. Once I went to the NFL Combine, I was going table to table interviewing with different coaches. I went to the next table and there he is. He was coaching with the San Diego Chargers at the time, so I knew I wasn't getting drafted there. I wish I would have took the time to thank everybody who gave me an opportunity, not only because it was an opportunity of a lifetime to do that, but the coaches just rotate place to place. I feel like that's definitely one of the regrets I have."

Chapter 7

Rod Wright

Rodrique Wright was always the biggest kid in his age group.

Growing up in Alief, a Houston suburb just west of downtown outside of the loop, Wright attended Hastings High School. His size allowed him to see the field early and grow into one of the top recruits in the 2002 class. Wright was deemed a five-star prospect by multiple recruiting services and would go on to rank as the No. 119 overall recruit in history and the No. 2 overall prospect Texas ever signed, according to *247Sports*.

"I was always bigger than everybody," Wright said. "My senior year I was around 330 pounds. I'm way smaller than that now, and I was way smaller than that when I played at Texas. I've always been a big kid."

Despite being the biggest and one of the best players in his area, Wright didn't have his eyes much on the future. Though he received a few letters in high school, as was customary at the time, Wright really didn't know he had a future in college football. Ironically it was the greatest coach in the history of the game who first showed up to watch it.

"It probably had to start in recruiting," Wright said. "You hear growing up that the size you have and how you played in little league and middle school. Once you are in high school, coaches start showing up, and that's kind of when you see that it's really going to happen. The very first coach I remember was Nick Saban. He came to my practice when I was a junior, and sadly I didn't know who he was. I wasn't a big college football fan. I always watched the NFL, but I didn't really pay attention that much to college football at the time. Obviously now he's the greatest college football coach ever. I actually got to play for him when he ended up drafting me at the Dolphins, but when the letters came in and I started showing up on the recruiting sites, that's when I really knew."

Wright's first dreams were of playing in the NBA. His length and athleticism made him grow up dreaming of playing for the Houston Rockets, but his weight changed his trajectory. With the NFL in mind, Wright knew he'd have to go to college in order to play in the league, but he didn't know where that would be. Unlike most kids in Texas, Wright didn't grow up with visions of donning the burnt orange of Texas or the maroon and white of Texas A&M. There wasn't a school in the country he knew he'd like to play at, but he'd soon get an up-close look at the recruiting landscape through the lens of an elite prospect.

"I didn't have one," Wright said. "It's kind of different from a lot of kids. I wanted to play professional football, but I was also starting in basketball. I wanted to be in the NBA, but once I got to 300 plus, I thought my future was in pro football. I never really had the dream growing up that I wanted to play at a certain school. I knew I needed to go to college, and I guess I just skipped that in my mind and thought I was going to go professional."

That didn't mean that Wright was unfamiliar with the power programs around him. He had a cousin who played at Texas in the past, and he knew what the impact of the Longhorn logo was within the state lines.

"Of course I knew who they were," Wright said. "I knew Texas. I knew A&M. In school you'd always talk about those two teams. I was aware of who they were. My cousin Cedric Woodard played [at Texas] as a defensive lineman, so they kind of had a head start as I had someone in my family playing there. I just knew who they were, knew what they meant to this state, and knew what football meant in this state. They were somebody that I knew had a great reputation and a great fan base. Everything is bigger and better in Texas, and that's the first school you think of because it's The University of Texas. That kind of resonated with me."

Texas started to show interest in Wright during his junior season. Mack Brown's top recruiter at the time was Tim Brewster. Brewster would go on to create a name for himself as a rainmaker on the recruiting trail. Before Brewster, Wright and his family had a connection to Texas through former Longhorn strength and conditioning coach Jeff "Mad Dog" Madden.

"The first coach was probably Tim Brewster," Wright said. "That's who my area recruiter was. I never was there with Coach Brewster because when he got me in, he left. I can't remember where he went, but that was my first interaction with a coach. Now my mom and Mad Dog's wife knew each other before we went to Texas. Mad Dog's wife when he was at Rice was a hairdresser in Houston, and my mom randomly used to go to her. When he went to Texas, we knew who they were, and they knew who I was. It was kind of one of those random type of deals. He wasn't really involved in the recruiting process before I went on the visit, but he was also part of the process as well."

Early in his recruiting process, Wright determined he wanted to stay in the state of Texas. His decision was twofold. For one, he wanted his family close so they could see his games and he could visit home from Austin. More than that, Wright wanted to stay in Texas and represent his home state on the field. He did look into schools in bordering states, but he wasn't considering the national powers at the time.

"I put it out there early that I wanted to stay in the state," Wright said. "Schools kind of knew that, and even though I put that out there, I still spoke with OU and LSU. There were a few other out-of-state schools. I got a lot of offers, but I really didn't entertain much outside of those schools. Really the top schools were Texas, Texas A&M, OU, and LSU. Outside of that, other schools called, but I can't remember giving attention to many other people other than just being polite. It was a combination of wanting to stay close to home so my family could see me and I could see them. I also wanted to as a Texas player—I just had a mindset early of keeping the talent at home. I even remember shortly considering the University of Houston, but at the time I didn't feel they had an opportunity to be on the level of winning a national championship, so that kind of killed it. For a person that didn't really tune into college football much until I was recruited, I did have a vision of winning a national championship in Texas and wanting to stay in Texas. It just made sense to me. We had the best talent, and if we kept all the best guys home and at the same place, there was no reason we couldn't win it all."

Wright's recruitment went smoothly. He visited Texas after his senior season on the weekend of their annual football banquet. That week was big for the Texas group that would go on to be ranked as the top recruiting class in the country. Wright was a big domino to fall for Brown, but he wouldn't be the last.

"I committed in December of 2001," Wright said. "I went to the big recruiting visit when everybody was kind of done with high school ball. The Houston Touchdown Club awards were on a Wednesday or Thursday that same week. I went on the visit that weekend, and a lot of the guys in the '02 class were at that visit. I ended up committing that Sunday."

Vince Young would be the biggest recruit for Texas in that cycle, but he hadn't yet committed. A player who would change the course of history for the Texas football program, Young was a Houston high school legend. Before Young was committed to Texas, the idea started to form at that Houston Touchdown Club dinner.

"That was before V.Y. committed," Wright said. "I actually met V.Y. for the first time at the Touchdown Club. I remember meeting with him and sitting down outside, and we had a grown man conversation at a young age of having similar mindsets about keeping the best talent in the state. We traded phone numbers, and I told him I was going to visit, and I'd let him know what I felt about the place. I went up there and had a great time. I called him after and told him about how I committed and now it was time for him. I didn't really have to recruit him much. I think me and Vince were on the same page. We were entertaining a lot of things, but I think we knew that's where we were going to go at the end of the day."

Though Wright was one of the players trying to get Young to join him at Texas, he didn't experience the same during his recruitment. In today's age recruits are connected constantly through social media, but that wasn't happening back then. Very few high school kids had cell phones at the time, and Wright wasn't big on putting himself out there.

"I was probably a little bit unreachable," Wright said. "I went to the Mack Brown Texas camp, and that was the first time I went around there. I wasn't big on going to unofficial visits. I literally went to the Nike Camp, the Mack Brown camp, and I went to the Red River Shootout—that's the only game I ever went to. I knew right then that this was what I needed to be a part of. It was the legendary game where Roy Williams jumped over the pile and sacked Chris Simms in the end zone. I actually had a feeling inside to go to Texas at that time and [turn] it around. I wasn't really someone I feel like a lot of people tried to call and sway me, but most of that was because I wasn't really on the circuit. I wasn't really around much."

Wright's visit to the Texas-OU game opened his eyes to being part of an intense rivalry unmatched in many other locations. The ironic part is that Wright attended the game as a guest of Oklahoma. As a neutral-site game, teams alternate home and away each year. In a given year only the home team can invite recruits and give out free tickets to attend. Texas and OU would trade blows for four quarters in a defensive struggle. With the score at 7–3 late in the game and Texas backed up to their own end zone, Oklahoma safety Roy Williams made an iconic play, flying over the line to strip Texas quarterback Chris Simms. The ball went up in the air, and Oklahoma linebacker Teddy Lehman caught it and scored. Oklahoma won 14–3 and should have benefitted on the recruiting front. While they went on to sign a talented class, Wright would not be part of it. Oddly enough, the result of the day opened Wright's eyes to the potential of what the Texas program could be.

"It blew my mind how intense it was," Wright said. "The crazy thing is, I went to the game as an OU recruit. I'm pretty unorthodox in that I went as an OU recruit, sat on their side, and watched them beat Texas—I should be convinced to go to OU. That's not where I wanted to go. I felt it was close, and instead of going with the team that won the game or the national championship, I was crazy enough to feel I was going to be a part of turning it around. It took me three years to do it because I lost to them three years in a row. My senior year we did it. Going to that game was outstanding, and I saw enough in Texas to think that they could get over the hump. I wasn't looking at OU being complete. I just felt the game was intense. Texas that year, if they beat Colorado in the Big 12 Championship, they are going to the national championship to play Miami. I saw enough to feel like I could help get them over the hump. That's how it felt watching them lose that game. I wanted to be a part of that game. I was excited about it, and every Red River game I played, I played well. It was a game I was always ready for."

Wright was hosted on his visit by defensive end Kalen Thornton. As was customary during the Mack Brown era, other players joined in and assisted on the recruiting side. Texas stars Marcus Tubbs and Cory Redding also spent time with him during the trip letting him know they wanted him to be part of the team.

"Kalen Thornton was my host," Wright said. "Through Kalen Thornton, Marcus Tubbs, and Cory Redding closing the deal, it was kind of the whole defensive line that took me under their wing. In my mind I always feel like Cory Redding was my host, but it was just because he jumped over and became a part of it. Even though Kalen was my host, I felt Tubbs and I felt Cory. It's kind of like what I feel we have here at UTSA [The University of Texas at San Antonio]. We have a real brotherhood where our kids take over. The best recruiting tool was the players. When you have that, it means they really do like where they are at. Players can feel that—recruits can feel that if guys are really opening their arms to others. I felt that family vibe of guys actually wanting me to be a part of their team."

The trip was his first time in Austin. Texas A&M was a school he considered early given College Station's proximity to Houston. Wright didn't feel that College Station was a fit for him, but Austin was another story.

"I hadn't been to Austin," Wright said. "I remember going to College Station, and A&M had a shot early. It was a little closer to Houston, but I just didn't like College Station, especially when you compare it to Austin and just being in the city. I'm from Houston, so I felt it was closer to me in the city and there were more things to do. Austin was great. There was a lot to do. It made me comfortable. You're right downtown. Austin now is a totally different place than when I was there, but I loved Austin. Most of our guys live there. When they are done, they move to Austin. You've got Houston guys and Dallas guys and guys from all over the state who come back to live in Austin. It's just different."

In his heyday there was nobody better at getting the commitment than Brown. Wright learned that lesson firsthand on his trip. When he went to Austin, he wasn't planning on committing. He still had a trip to LSU planned before he would make his final decision, but Brown didn't want to take the chance of losing him. When Wright stepped into his office at the conclusion of the visit, he didn't know that he would be facing an ambush from Brown with an assist from his own parents.

"I did not intend to commit," Wright said. "I took it all the way until the end of the trip. I was the last guy Coach Brown saw. We stayed in his office for hours. He was trying to do his best pitch, and I told him, 'I'm not committing.' It wasn't because I didn't want to go there, but I planned on going on the visit to LSU next week. I was going to stick to the script because I already set the visit. Coach Brown told me he'd leave me and my parents alone to talk about it. It was kind of weird because I told him I wasn't going to commit. I never really asked my parents about it, but he probably felt my parents giving him the under-the-table agreement they'd get me to come. He went into the other offices, and there was a staff meeting going on in the staff room connected to his office. I told them that we were going to tell Coach Brown that we weren't going to commit, but as soon as I started talking to my parents, they started recruiting me to Texas. They started talking about getting it done now and how they weren't going on the visit with me the next week. They told me, 'Let's commit and go to the bookstore and buy you a shirt.' I felt betrayed for a little bit. They convinced me, and Coach Brown came back in. I told him I was going to commit, and he took me into the staff room. I told the staff I was going to commit, and they all jumped up and high-fived and everything. I really wasn't going to commit until my parents flipped the script. If they didn't do that, I would have walked out of there without committing. That's no shade on Coach Brown, but he didn't get me, he got my parents. So give them the credit for doing the recruiting that day."

It was on that trip that Wright became well acquainted with Brown. The man who would become his head coach hit all of the right notes during that official visit. Now a college coach himself, Wright sharpened his recruiting skills with the same blueprint Brown used for him.

"It was probably on the official visit," Wright said. "We can talk on the phone all day and you can write letters, but until I see you face-to-face and see you around me and my family and other players, you could tell this dude does value me. I remember on that trip being the last guy in the office and they took me and showed me the depth chart. Maybe they showed the depth chart to everybody, but I know that's a sacred board. He showed me where I would fit and how they'd use me. I knew that I was somebody that he wanted there, and that kind of spoke to me. The way he is with moms and dads—he makes every parent feel comfortable leaving their child with him. Still today as I recruit now, I have a big place in my heart for parents because I experienced that. I know how comfortable Coach Brown and all the folks at Texas made my folks feel. They delivered too. It wasn't one of those deals where they said something and it was something else. It was exactly what they said it was."

No Texas visit was complete without the involvement of Sally Brown. Mack's wife was mentioned by every player we spoke with, and Wright felt she was a perfect fit in a program that constantly preached family values.

"She's just the mom," Wright said. "She's a sweet soul, and she always has a smile on her face. She'd make you feel welcome. She's one of those people who probably never said a cuss word in her life. She was great. It was the type of program where you felt everybody had your back. Even though it's football, you feel like they cared about you more than just on the field. They cared about you academically and where you were going to go after football."

Wright would go on to play in the U.S. Army All-American Bowl with a large group of commits from the Texas class. The group became close and formed a bond that would one day lead to a national championship.

"We had a bond," Wright said. "After that official visit, everybody traded numbers. We had the No. 1 class, and right then and there we sealed the deal. We were the best class ever and all that. We believed in it. We wore it with confidence. That Army Bowl, there was a lot of Texas guys on that team. We won that game, and that was pretty cool. That was kind of the warm-up. I know V.Y. was there. Justin Blalock was there. Aaron Harris was there. Kasey Studdard was there. We had a good amount of guys there."

In today's game it's expected that recruits will report to campus for the first semester of summer school in June to begin workouts with the team ahead of fall camp. In 2002 it was up to the players whether they wanted to train on their own or come in early. Wright opted to stay at home in Houston. That spring, Wright inched closer to 350 pounds, but he knew he would need to come in much lighter if he wanted a chance to play early. Players receive a manual for workouts after signing with their desired school. Wright went to work on the book that Madden sent him and shed the weight.

"Back then you had a choice of if you wanted to enroll in the summer and train with the team or do it on your own," Wright said. "I did not train with the team. It's crazy, but I took that book Mad Dog gave me and I went to work. I lost weight. That's the reason I played as a true freshman. At the spring game, I want to say I was like 342 pounds, and I reported to camp at 305. Nobody knew I dropped that much weight. As I think about it, I couldn't imagine a freshman of mine being 330 and showing up to camp at 305 looking like a different person. I couldn't imagine it. I ate better. I trained using the book. I did the running and did the lifting to the best of my ability, and I came in ready to go. I really think that's why I was successful there. We had jobs, though. We worked in the summer. I worked at a plant doing assistant work—it was almost like being a secretary. We just did what they asked and did whatever they asked us to do."

Wright saw what Young could do from afar living in Houston at the same time Young was turning heads in the city. Wright became well acquainted with Young's skills once he arrived in Austin.

"It was amazing," Wright said. "I knew that guy was legit. The way he ran and the way he threw it. His size and everything was impressive. Being in Houston, I really got to see who he was, and the city embraced him."

Wright saw the field almost immediately. He played in all 13 games that season and started 9 games, earning first-team All-America honors. He followed it up with a strong effort in 2003, leading the team in sacks with 7.5 and 35 pressures. Wright and Texas found themselves on the short end of the conference while Oklahoma continuously came out on top. Even after Oklahoma, Texas usually stumbled and lost another game or two each year. These missteps kept Texas from reaching the heights they were shooting for.

"The conference always went through Oklahoma," Wright said. "We'd always drop a game to Tech or drop a game to Arkansas. It was always disappointing. We knew we shouldn't lose games to anyone. We knew the one game we had to get right was OU, but dropping games to other teams—we got that fixed my junior year. The only game we lost was to OU. We knew we were there and knew we were close."

In 2004 Wright once again found himself on that Cotton Bowl field fighting Oklahoma for control of the conference. Texas came out on the short end that game with a 12–0 defeat at the hands of their rivals to the north. It was the fifth straight loss Texas would concede to their rivals, but Wright and the team knew they were capable of more.

"It wasn't down," Wright said. "It was 6–0 for most of the game, and we knew we'd lost that game but knew we were right there. We left that game knowing we were better. We knew the offense wouldn't get shut out like that again and the defense was very confident. We played the heck out of their offense, and they were really good. They went to the national championship. We knew that was a good team, and we looked on the schedule and knew there wasn't another game that we should lose."

Texas won out after losing to Oklahoma and was selected to play in the Rose Bowl against Michigan. The Longhorns and Brown were criticized as a team and a coach who couldn't win the big one. Facing a tough Michigan team that featured a ton of future-NFL talent, Texas narrowly won 38–37 on a last-second field goal.

"It was a big deal," Wright said. "That was the game where we'd been out of the BCS, and the question was if Texas could ever win a big game like that. We were playing Michigan—a historic university—and it was a big stage. The biggest stage of our careers at that point. It was a big-time game. It was very physical. It was an NFL game, basically, with the amount of talent in it."

During the trophy presentation after the game, Young boldly stated that the Longhorns would be back to the Rose Bowl the following year, where the BCS National Championship would be played. Young's big wager would pay off, and the Longhorns knew they had what it took to win it all the next year.

"We knew," Wright said. "I always tell people that it started with the 2004 season. The turnaround of Texas football was that season when

Greg Robinson and Dick Tomey came in with an old-school mentality and the confidence of a Super Bowl champion in Greg Robinson. They came in and installed a toughness, and we went back to the old school. We were a tough team. We were mentally tough and physically tough, and that's where we became a championship-caliber team. When Vince said we were going to go back, that's all we had left to do. We proved we could win a big BCS game and all we had to do was beat OU."

Player-led teams are the strongest of any teams in sports. The losing wore on the roster, and they made their minds up following that season to do whatever it takes. Wright was part of a strong core that led the team.

"It was really strong," Wright said. "It started my junior year, and after the 2003 season, we lost to Washington State in the Holiday Bowl. That left a really bitter taste in our mouths. There is nothing worse than losing to a team you feel like you should beat. We kind of got over that, and we got tired of losing. It wasn't about us winning, we were just tired of losing. We were tired of losing to OU and tired of losing games we knew we should win. Leadership just kind of took over. That's why my big belief now is I can coach and say whatever I want to say, but it's up to a player to make his mind up. We made our minds up to hit it hard and take it serious. We were at 7-on-7 in the summer. It still wasn't everyone in the summer like it is now. That was a decision that needed to be made, and we made that decision."

Following the 2004 season, defensive coordinator Greg Robinson was hired by Syracuse to be their next head coach. Brown brought in Auburn's Gene Chizik to replace him. Chizik was the hottest name of any assistant on the market, and he found himself in charge of a veteran defense ready to take out their frustrations on college football.

"He brought a lot of confidence," Wright said. "When Greg Robinson left, it was going to be our third DC in three years. When he came in, one of the first things he said resonated with all of us. He said that the Big 12 title was going to be had, and I think everybody felt that and everybody believed that. We were a motivated team, and I really believe it didn't matter who they brought in. Our minds were made up, and that's no discredit to Gene. This is what we wanted, and this is what we were going to do. When he came in he had the confidence, and we had a veteran team. We didn't have to beg anybody to be anywhere. We were ready. He came in with his confidence and his swagger and demeanor, and he also had a toughness about him. It was a perfect fit."

For Texas to reach their dreams, they'd have to get through a tough early-season matchup with Ohio State. The Horseshoe is the home of the Buckeyes and one of the most hostile environments in all of collegiate sports. Trained by years of hostility in the Texas-OU matchup, the Longhorns had no problem handling what the Buckeye fans gave them.

"It was great," Wright said. "It don't get more hostile than the Red River Rivalry, in all honesty. That's the best environment, so it wasn't anything we weren't prepared for. It was outstanding. There were a lot of great players. I met a lot of them at the Playboy All-American deal. Me and Jonathan Scott had already met Ted Ginn [Jr.] and Santonio Holmes [Jr.] and A.J. Hawk. When we went there, that's when I realized how good those guys would be. We were just ready for the moment. It was a really intense game, but, like I said, the mindset that we had and the mental toughness we had, we were just ready. We just knew how to win. We knew that no matter what, at the end of the game, we'd get the stops and the offense would get the scores. That was a big test early that gave us the confidence to know that we were a force to be reckoned with."

The conference always went through Dallas and the Red River Shootout. Texas entered the game looking to finally get a win and break a five-year losing streak that plagued them over and over. Texas exorcised all kinds of demons, defeating Oklahoma 45–12. The exclamation came in the fourth quarter when Brian Robison crushed Oklahoma quarterback Rhett Bomar, causing a fumble. Wright scooped it up and ran 67 yards for a score.

"It was one of those dream plays," Wright said. "We were putting the whooping on them, and they had a drive going. They slid to the boundary and let Brian right off the edge. I guess Rhett was supposed to get that ball off and never did. When I felt it slide, I popped the protection and went outside so it was almost like he went down and I went out. I come around, and that ball popped right into my hands. I just took off and thought it was going to be one of those plays where they blow the whistle in like 10 or 15 yards. I didn't hear a whistle and just kept going. Next thing you know, I was in the end zone. It was one of those moments where you just don't believe it's real. At that point in time we knew we were going to win that game. It was over, and that was the exclamation mark. It's something that, when you think of the game, you think of that play. It was something that I was very excited to do because it put an end to a long drought and put us in a situation where we were in the driver's seat."

In a documentary the Longhorn Network produced about the 2005 season, Young called the score the "slowest touchdown ever." Wright said he couldn't even believe it.

"I know there were a lot of big-man jokes and a lot of slow jokes," Wright said. "I just didn't think it was real until it was real. It was cool, man. It was big time. I was like, 'Just keep running.' I didn't think about getting caught. I didn't think about how long it was. I just said to myself,

'Go until they blow the whistle.' I really thought they were going to blow the whistle, but when it never happened, I just kept going."

With Oklahoma out of the way, it looked like a clear path to Pasadena and a date with destiny. A 5–5 Texas A&M team looked to play spoiler and gave Texas the biggest scare of the season. The Longhorns would prevail in a 40–29 victory, with Wright making a game-saving play forcing a turnover when the Aggies were driving late.

"The biggest play I ever made was really in the A&M game," Wright said. "A&M was driving to go take the lead, and we are in the red zone. I got a sack-fumble there and that kind of changed the game. If they scored there, they'd probably win because they had momentum the entire game. That was a play that I remember making a play and getting the ball back. Keeping them from scoring on us was a big deal, but that game was a big scare. A lot of times, especially in college, it's not as good as you think it is when the starting quarterback is out. When a good quarterback you don't know anything about is the starter, you're kind of screwed. He came in and was a dude. We turned it over a few times, and A&M played good defense. It's hard to play there, and I think it's just one of those classic rivalry games where they wanted to do everything to spoil our season. We just had to have that gut check to push through and get into the championship game."

Texas discarded Colorado with a 70–3 win in the Big 12 title game. They would finally reach their dream of playing for a national championship, but the Longhorns would have to contend with a USC team that was being hailed as the greatest of all time. As the title game drew nearer the national media turned the game into a David-and-Goliath matchup against a USC team that nobody could possibly beat.

"That's all we heard," Wright said. "All year it was about how great they were [and] everything that came with it. We felt like it was over before it was over. I remember seeing an ESPN story of them talking about if they were the best team in college football history. That obviously resonated because they didn't think we had a chance to win that game. We definitely got tired of it because we knew how good we were. We knew what we had to work with. It was just one of those things where we had our shot, and it was great that they were sleeping on a really good team. We knew it would work in our advantage if they overlooked us."

Before Texas reached Pasadena, the postseason awards cycle saw them heavily recognized. Texas took home several major awards, but its brightest star couldn't win the biggest. Young was a finalist for the Heisman Trophy, but he lost to USC running back Reggie Bush in a massive landslide. Young's frustration was felt through the television screens broadcasting the ceremony, and he called Wright afterward to tell him to get the boys together and get ready to go to work. Wright was disappointed for his friend, but he knew what that disappointment would bring out in him when they reached Pasadena.

"I can only really speak for me," Wright said. "I knew who Vince was, and I knew what he was going to do in that game. I was disappointed for him, but once it happened, I knew what kind of Vince would show up at the game. It was a double-edged sword because he didn't win the Heisman, but we were going to go home with that national championship."

Though there were some nerves once Wright got to the field, the Longhorns knew they were prepared. They had been in the same stadium the year before and did everything exactly the same.

"Once you show up and it's really going down, I felt it then," Wright said. "To me, different individuals think differently. I didn't have many nerves until we got there. We did the trial run the year before. We stayed at the same hotel. We were on the same sideline wearing the same colors. In reality it was about as good as you could draw it up."

As the game progressed, both teams tilted back and forth for control. With 6:42 remaining in the fourth quarter, USC scored a touchdown to go up by 11. On the play, Texas defensive backs Tarell Brown and Michael Griffin collided. Both had to leave the game, and the outlook seemed bleak. Wright said that hope was the only thing left on the Texas sideline.

"It was hope," Wright said. "All we could have was hope that Vince would go and score and give us a second chance to get a score on defense. When I saw Mike and Tarell Brown go down, that was the one time in the game where I thought, 'This is why they are USC.' They went up by 12, and two of our best players got hurt on the same play. All we could do is hope that the offense could score and give us another shot. That was kind of the mood because it was out of our hands. You just kind of put your energy and focus on controlling what we could control. If we scored, we needed to be ready to get a stop. That was our one job, to then give them a chance to get back out there and give us the lead."

Young led the Longhorns down the field for a score to get the game within six points. Wright and the defense took the field with the aim of getting a stop and giving the offense one more chance to win it. The game came down to a fourth-and-2 play, and Heisman winner Reggie Bush was on the sideline. Texas stopped USC running back LenDale White, who had already run for 124 yards and three touchdowns.

"I didn't know he wasn't out there," Wright said. "I wasn't thinking about it. You're not better off, in my mind, either way. It's not like if Reggie is out, it gets easier. In that situation, LenDale was doing his thing and coming downhill. It was short yardage. You wouldn't necessarily think that if they run power, Reggie is going to bust through and get those two yards. I know I didn't think about it at all. There's too much going on. You've got to get lined up and get your call. You've got to go out there and get a stop to win the damn game. In my mind there wasn't much else to think about."

Texas went on to win after some late heroics by Young and the Texas offense. While everyone on the field celebrated, Wright breathed a sigh of relief.

"For me it was relief," Wright said. "From the day I got on campus, I was blessed to be in a position to compete to play. I had started my freshman year, and I went from a young guy playing early to an old guy playing late. I kind of saw us scratch and claw and knock on the door for three years. To finally get to my fourth year and win it all, it was a real moment. It was bigger than just that year. We hadn't won one since 1970, so we did something that hadn't been done in a long time and hasn't been done since. It's something that's hard to do. It was a weight off my shoulders and the feeling that we really did it. I was more excited in the other Rose Bowl. For one, we kicked it at the end, and you had the feeling of the final play, but this one was just like a peaceful feeling that we did it."

Wright was selected in the seventh round of the 2006 NFL Draft by the Miami Dolphins. Between the NFL and the CFL, Wright played five professional seasons before retiring. When he returned to Texas to finish his degree, he got his foot in the door with an eye toward his future.

"I wanted to stay close to the game," Wright said. "At first I wanted to be a commentator after I was done playing ball. I knew I wanted to be around the game, and at some point it switched to coaching. The first time I thought about coaching, it was in high school, and a coach was running the hell out of us after practice. I remember thinking that it's nice to watch other people run and just yell at them, and I joke that it was my first thought of coaching. Obviously I was just being lazy and didn't want to run, but that was kind of my first thought. I just felt I could stay involved in the game. I know how to play and how to lead. I knew how to network and who I would call to be my references. I knew all these coaches, and it just made great sense. This is what I've done, and the network is going to continue to give to me because of all the people I know and how I carry myself. I started out thinking I'd be a high school coach. I was done with the NFL much faster than I would like. I went back to finish my college degree because I left a semester early to train for the league. When I went back in, Mack was still there. I asked him if he would allow me to watch spring ball because I wanted to coach, and he allowed me to. That was the beginning of my coaching career, going out with my own shorts and shirt and watching Coach Giles and Bo Davis coach the defensive line. I was actually still in the CFL, so I went there after spring ball and got cut. I played in one game in the Arena League and got cut. That's when I knew it was over. I went back to Texas to finish one more semester, and Coach Brown put me on the staff as a student coach. That's where it went from there."

After stints at Sam Houston State University and East Carolina University, Wright had the opportunity to return to Texas for a position with The University of Texas at San Antonio. He spent three years with the Roadrunners before moving to Miami in the spring of 2022. Being on the other side of the table, Wright brings his own element to recruiting.

"Players are looking for real," Wright said. "There's levels to this if a guy is a power-five guy or a big-time guy—at UTSA we have big-time guys, but there's a dynamic. If a guy is only talking to the Texases and the Alabamas and Georgias, nowadays we still talk to them because the portal is so crazy. There's a great chance once he enters the portal, he'd remember you. My first on-field job was at Sam Houston State. The only chance I had was relationships. No disrespect to Sam Houston, but people don't just wake up and say, 'I'm going to play at Sam Houston.' A lot of times we were people that they respected, but we weren't the first choice. A lot of times we just had to have a relationship with them. Now…it's what I do. I never had a kid I didn't relate to or understand what they want. They want to see real. At the end of the day, every coach says what they are going to say, but what makes them real or unique? I always tell them that because I'm an ex-player, I know what it's like. I've been recruited by the best. I feel like I have an advantage because I was recruited by Mack Brown. I feel like I know how to do it because I was recruited by the guys who were the best at what they did."

Wright worked under UTSA head coach Jeff Traylor. A former Texas high school coach, Traylor was an important mentor for Wright in his young career.

"Jeff's been amazing to learn under," Wright said. "[We] are really a lot alike. He's about family. He's a lot like Mack Brown in the sense of wanting to create a family atmosphere, wanting to be real, and wanting to be authentic. He'll tell you what he's going to tell you. Of course you have to sell yourself and sell the university, but he may say something that will lose a kid by telling him the truth. We may lose a kid, but he will come back if it doesn't work out where he's at. It's been awesome. He does it the right way. He has the Texas high school coaches on his side, and he knows this state better than anybody. That's important to me because I've only coached one year out of the state. I've been in this state and recruited it for a long time. I have a lot of relationships. For him, being who he is and what he means to this state is a huge advantage in recruiting."

With his playing career behind him and his coaching career in front of him, Wright doesn't have any regrets about how everything played out.

"I really can't say I have any," Wright said. "I was really green coming in, and I liked that because I was able to see it from a real lens. I wasn't born to be at Texas or born to be at A&M. I guess some people would say they would want to take a bunch of visits, but when you know, you know—and I knew. I knew where I wanted to be, and I didn't want to waste anybody's time. I've been doing this for a while now, and you know when kids don't want to be there but they still court you. It's just a waste of time. Players have to play the game. We're recruiting a million people and you're talking to a million people. I get it. These coaches have families and any time we are talking to a recruit or with a recruit, we are away from our families. I'm sure those coaches were disappointed I didn't come to their university, but I didn't waste their time either. I let them know I wasn't going to come and all that after I committed. If I would have been on a trip and out there faking it, it would have been a waste of their time. I really don't have any regrets, especially with us winning a national championship. Obviously I wish we would have won every year, but that game was the greatest game because of the game itself and the storylines. There's no way to recreate Pete Carroll, Matt Leinart, Reggie Bush, Snoop Dogg, and Will

Ferrell at USC. You'll never recreate that monster. Two Heismans were on the same team, and the way they were moving was phenomenal. It was the greatest game because we dethroned them. Bama lost this year, but it wasn't Bama with all of the championships. It was a different Bama team. This USC team was stacked.

Then you have our storylines. We had Vince Young and the running backs, the offensive line, and the receivers. We had a top-ranked defense. We had awards and All-Americans. We had the No. 1 recruiting class and Mack Brown, a guy that everyone loved who couldn't quite get it done. The university that everyone loved and hated at the same time that couldn't get it done got it done against the best that ever did it. The storyline and the game being at the Rose Bowl played into it. If it was at the Fiesta Bowl or something like that, it wouldn't hit the same.

Everything lined up exactly as it should have. Games don't live up like that. That's why I always say that if I'd have won four national championships, it wouldn't come down to that storyline. I don't really have many regrets, but I do wish we were playing in the era where NIL [Name, Image, and Likeness] deals are where they are now. I'd probably be a lot richer, but it is what it is."

CHAPTER 8

Michael Huff

Michael Huff never planned on playing college football.

He thought his future was on the track. Huff ran in summer programs and for his school from the time he was a kindergartener. By the time he reached high school at Nimitz High School in the Dallas suburb of Irving, Huff was one of the most talented sprinters in his class. Though he played well on the football field for the Nimitz Vikings, Huff was preparing to accept a track-and-field scholarship to the University of Houston. The program that produced U.S. track-and-field legend Carl Lewis was one of the most prestigious in the nation, and Huff's future pointed more toward the Olympics than the Rose Bowl.

"Early on, all I cared about was track," Huff said. "I was a big track guy growing up. I started running track when I was five. For me, the first love was track. I just played football because you played down in the IBFA [Irving Boys Football Association] down in the river bottoms where the fields were back then. I played just to play because every little kid played. For me, I probably didn't think I would play college football until my senior year. It wasn't like nowadays where you get offers your freshman year or sophomore year. For me, I didn't get a Texas offer until I went and visited them in mid-December when I officially got the offer. During that whole time, I thought I was going to go to college to run track. Football-wise I knew I was good, but I never dreamed of playing at the next level."

Though he grew up in Irving, Huff and his family grew up watching the Michigan Wolverines on television each week. One reason for that was his family ties to the state, but Wolverine defensive back Charles Woodson captured Huff's focus on the field. The Wolverines never entered the picture for Huff, but if they had, his story would have been completely different.

"Charles Woodson and my mom and dad were born in Muskegon, [Michigan]," Huff said. "It was right there outside of Detroit, so we grew up watching nothing but Michigan Wolverines football. I knew I wasn't going up there because it was too cold—Michigan would have been it though. I feel like if they would have offered, I would have went there. I'd have dealt with the cold weather and that side of it. At that time if I had a Michigan offer, I'd have gone there after Texas. I was born and raised in Texas, but everything we watched was the Detroit Lions, Barry Sanders, and Michigan football with Charles Woodson. We didn't watch the Cowboys. For me growing up, I was a Woodson fan and everyone else was a Deion [Sanders] fan. To this day I'm still a Woodson fan."

It was all Michigan all the time in the Huff household. The family never watched any of the college Texas teams, and the Longhorns might as well have been on another planet.

"I didn't watch any Texas football growing up," Huff said. "When I say that, I mean I didn't watch any college teams in Texas. I watched the Cowboys on Thanksgiving Day after the Lions, but as far as UT football, I never watched it growing up. It was all just Michigan. If we didn't watch Michigan, we didn't watch anything at all. I wasn't really familiar with Jerry Gray and the great defensive backs that came from Texas before [me]. Growing up, Texas football didn't exist."

Late in his senior season, Purdue showed interest in Huff as a wide receiver recruit. Huff played both ways, but his only experience at receiver was in a run-heavy Wing-T offense at Nimitz. In his role as a wide receiver, Huff mostly lined up in a three-point stance and ran very few routes. Outside of Purdue, most of his interest was in track.

"Purdue was really it," Huff said. "We had U of H and Arkansas, but that was for track. For me, it was more track, and I could walk-on and go play football. Football was really just Purdue and Texas when they offered."

Texas came along late in the process. Defensive ends coach Hardee McCrary had a link to Nimitz through Nimitz head coach Mike Farda. The two went back a long way, and Texas was looking for a developmental prospect with tools. Huff's size and speed made him a desirable candidate for long-term development.

"It was all Hardee McCrary," Huff said. "I didn't talk to Coach [Duane] Akina or anyone like that until I got on the visit. I guess Hardee was great friends with Mike Farda, my old head coach. Hardee went to bat for me that if I could play for Mike Farda, I was a tough guy, and they knew I could run. They thought I might be a good special teams player. He knew being coached by Mike Farda, I was a good player and person. Without Coach Farda and Coach Hardee, I probably would have never been at Texas."

Huff was invited on an official visit in late December after his football season was over. He was hosted on the trip by several Texas players and was able to see the family atmosphere that made Texas recruiting so successful.

"It was either Nathan Vasher or Rod Babers," Huff said. "Back then we all hung out with each other. On the visit, it was Kendal Briles and Cedric Griffin, and we were all on the visit together. They kept all of the defensive backs together. For me, I think it was either Babers or Vasher that was my host. The brotherhood stood out, as far as the players. You had the guys like Cory Redding, Casey Hampton [Jr.], Shaun Rogers, and Leonard Davis. They were all there. It wasn't like I was just this little two-star defensive back recruit. It was all of the guys. We went to a place called Drinks—that was our little spot back then. We were all with each other the whole time, and you could truly tell it was more of a player-led program. It was just a brotherhood. Everyone was just in the dorms together and the locker room together, and on my visit, you could truly feel that."

Mack Brown offered Huff during the visit. As a late addition to the class, he had never talked with the Texas head coach. Most of his contact was directly through McCrary, who served as the area recruiter, and Huff was intimidated in his meeting with Brown. Once the offer was on the table, Brown pushed for an immediate commitment. Without many other options, Huff committed right then and there.

"I was scared of Mack when I first got there," Huff said. "As soon as I went in his office and they gave me the offer, they asked me if I was coming or not. It was right then at that moment I had to commit. There was no time to wait and think about this or that. Obviously I didn't have any other places I was going, so I knew I had to say yes. I committed on the spot. Mack is a politician. When you get in the room with Mack, he could sell a dream to anybody. Obviously that's a good thing. He could really sell the program and everything he's going to do."

While on the visit, Huff also met defensive backs coach Duane Akina. Akina would become a strong figure in Huff's life and would shape his development on the football field. Meeting Akina on the visit and speaking with his players, Huff was able to get a feel for the way the coach cared about his players. Once he enrolled at Texas, he'd get a firsthand lesson about Akina's teaching style. Huff came in with the reputation for not wanting to tackle or play physically. Akina recognized this immediately and worked with Huff every day on a pad by the pole vault pit. Huff would work at tackling from different angles as walk-on players served as victims. By the end of his career, Huff would be one of the best tacklers in college football.

"It was truly how he cared about his players," Huff said. "Obviously he had those defensive backs like Vasher, Babers, and [Quentin] Jammer. I asked them what they liked about Coach Akina, and they said he was the same person at 7:00 AM on an off-day as he is on game day when it's tied going into the fourth quarter. He's that fiery, intense guy. He's going to love you up, but everybody has different buttons, and he knows which ones to push for each person to get them going. That's one thing I truly loved about him. I was a skinny track guy, so, for me, I had to go down to the pits every day after practice and just tackle walk-ons. It was just tackling every day because that was my Achilles' heel. I didn't want to hit anybody. He told me that if I never learned how to tackle, I'd never play a down there, and I could truly tell he meant it. He took me down to the pits every day, so it's not like he told me that and left me to the side. He told me, and he showed me what to do. We'd go watch film on it and do little things like that. It seemed like a one-on-one experience, but he was like that with everybody."

No experience during this era was complete without a Sally Brown story. Like many others, Huff was impacted by Sally's mark on the program. The First Lady of Texas football left a lasting legacy.

"We loved Sally," Huff said. "You can ask anyone, and everybody loved her. She was just that one person that I haven't seen since. She truly embedded herself in the program. You could tell that we were her children. Every plane ride she'd make cookies for us. She was at every event regardless of what was going on. Every Thursday she was at practice. She was around all the time. She'd make cookies and cakes and send you letters if you got a good grade in class. For us, she truly was the First Lady, and I think that's why everyone responded to her and loved her."

When Huff was offered, not even his father could believe it. Huff was still raw from a football perspective. Though the offer was a surprise, Huff's parents weren't going to let him pass on the opportunity to be the first person in his family to graduate from college.

"The funny part is, as soon as they offered me, my dad kind of looked at me and then looked at Coach Akina and asked if they were sure," Huff said. "I always joke with [Texas sports information director] John Bianco because Coach Akina and Coach Brown told him that story. They were so surprised to get that reaction from a parent. Obviously my dad loved me, but he was surprised I was good enough to go to Texas. That was kind of my dad's first reaction. We were all shocked and surprised. Even though I had an official, there was no inkling of anything. I didn't talk to Coach Akina or Coach Brown before that. There was no guarantee I was going to get an offer. They just took me down there for a weekend. Once we got the offer, my parents were happy. They wanted me to be the first one to graduate from college. They'd be happy if I went anywhere, just as long as I was the first one to graduate from college, so they were supportive."

Huff waited to enroll until late in the summer so he could compete in his final track season. Though a hamstring injury kept him from reaching the state meet, Huff was able to make a deep run in his final year. He came to Austin as a lowly recruit rated with two stars, but Huff made up his mind to do everything possible to become the best player in the defensive back room.

"The crazy part is, once I got to Texas, I knew football was it," Huff said. "I put all my eggs in one basket after being so focused on track. Things kind of flipped, and I kind of started to play with a chip on my shoulder. I came in with Cedric Griffin, Kendal Briles, Rufus Harris. I didn't know if Quan Cosby would be a defensive back or not, so, for me, I kind of looked at all of those guys and was just like, 'I'm going to be the best out of everybody.' That was just my mindset from the time I got on campus. Since we all redshirted, I knew we were all going to be on the same playing field coming out of the season and going into spring ball. I just wanted to work my ass off to be the best one in the group. That was just my mindset."

Huff redshirted during his first year and took the opportunity to learn from one of the best. Quentin Jammer was a senior on the team and would be selected in the top 10 of the NFL Draft the following year. In their short time together on campus, Huff absorbed everything he could from the elite cornerback.

"That was Quentin Jammer's senior year," Huff said. "He was a [Jim] Thorpe [Award] finalist. He was the one that kind of set the tone for us. Just us seeing him play at a high level and how he worked every day and seeing the leader he was off the field. For me, he was the perfect example of what an elite guy in that room is supposed to be on and off the field. I wouldn't be the player I ended up being without Quentin Jammer setting that example. He wasn't a loud rah-rah guy. I'm not either, but he led by example, and when he did speak up, everybody listened. For me, he was the perfect example, and I kind of latched on to him for the six months or so that I was with him before he went to the NFL. That redshirt year, from when I got there in the summer until January when he left, that was the best thing for me."

Huff got on the field early, playing both cornerback and safety. Though he'd play early at corner, where the bulk of his high school experience was, Huff was moved to safety. He didn't have much experience there, but he saw it as an opportunity to get on the field. From there, Huff set about mastering the roles of several players on the defense and pairing his elite speed with an enhanced mental approach to the game. That mindset kept him on the field and led to him playing in 51 games and starting in 50.

"At that point I just wanted to be on the field," Huff said. "I just knew whatever it took to get on the field I would do it. My freshman year, I think I started 10 games at safety and 3 games at corner. I still got to play corner and safety, and I'd move inside and play the nickel. I knew with that versatility it would help me out in the long run if I did end up playing at the next level. Going into spring it was my goal to learn every position on the back end. I learned what the linebackers were doing in case we went to nickel or dime. For me, the football IQ part of the game is the one that I knew where I could have a step up on the rest of the defensive backs. A lot of defensive backs don't care about the mental side of the game, but, for me, I knew that's how you'd get an advantage. Things slow down and it makes the game a lot easier when you focus on that mental part."

During his time on campus, Huff started in four matchups against Oklahoma. The Red River Shootout held each October is one of the best settings in all of college football. It was as a player where Huff realized how special and volatile the environment was.

"It was the craziest environment I've ever been in," Huff said. "I never got to go to something like Michigan–Ohio State. I didn't go to college football games period, so just being in that rivalry game, I was kind of shell-shocked. I was back at home in Dallas, but you run out of the tunnel, and it's half orange and half them. As the game goes, there's just mood swings. I still feel like the majority of the time in that game, we had the better team. In that game, you never know what's going to happen with the momentum. You never know which players are going to make those iconic plays. In that game, you never knew what was going to happen regardless of the record or the rankings—that environment and how it is, I wasn't ready for it in my early years."

Huff came to Texas at the end of the Chris Simms and Major Applewhite era. As he grew into an upperclassman, Huff watched the development of legendary Texas quarterback Vince Young. Early on, the talent of Young oozed every time he touched the ball, but his development didn't come without growing pains.

"We definitely knew talent-wise who he was, what he could be, and what he could turn this place into," Huff said. "I think early on his career, especially when he was battling with Chance Mock, we had one offense. It was built for guys like Chance, but when Vince went in there, they tried to make him a pocket passer. They didn't let him be creative and be Vince. Early on, you could tell he was just out of his element. We saw him in practice where he couldn't run around and scramble, and he'd sit in the pocket and try to read defenses. You could definitely tell he was struggling, and at one point he was ready to transfer when he was redshirting. He didn't want to be there. He went through a lot, but he stuck it out and talked to Mack. Long term it worked out, but he obviously went through some struggles. In high school he was the man, so I'm sure he expected to walk on campus and do the same thing."

During Huff's junior season, Texas found themselves in familiar territory. A midseason loss to Oklahoma—the fifth loss in a row to their rival to the north—threatened to spike their season again. Little did Huff and the rest of the team know, they wouldn't lose a game again for almost two years.

"We really just went back to work," Huff said. "We knew what kind of team we had and the talent we had, and everything was out there in front of us. I think we just put our head back down and went to work, and we'd see what happened at the end of the year. We knew we still had one loss."

The 2004 season culminated in a Rose Bowl bid against Michigan. The game held special meaning for Huff. Growing up watching Michigan win huge games in the most fabled setting in collegiate sports, Huff's family would watch him suit up opposite the Wolverines in the big game.

"For me, it was surreal," Huff said. "Playing against Michigan, a team I loved growing up, and then doing it at the Rose Bowl where Michigan had played so many big games. That's where Charles Woodson had the one-handed pick on the sideline. Those moments that were in that stadium—and I was in that stadium playing against Michigan seeing the Maize and Blue. I definitely got the shivers. I was one of the first ones out there. As the game went on, I kind of calmed down, but it was cool. Especially for my parents, who were such die-hard Michigan fans. It was special for them to see me get to play against them and come out with a win against them."

The game was loaded with talent on both sides of the ball. Aside from Oklahoma, Texas would rarely see a team as talented as Michigan was that year, and the big-game environment would prepare them for what was to come the next season.

"Back then we'd play Oklahoma State, who might have one or two guys," Huff said. "Obviously OU always had their guys, but it wasn't a roster full of NFL talent week after week. You looked at Michigan and then Ohio State the next year. Obviously USC the next year. We didn't see those types of games every week. I think that Michigan victory helped us go into the Horseshoe [Ohio State's stadium] and win against Ohio State. It helped us beat USC in the national championship. Without the Michigan game, I feel like we wouldn't be prepared for the next season."

Texas won 38–37 on a game-ending field goal. With only a few players leaving that year, Huff and company knew they had the capacity to do something special the next year.

"We knew," Huff said. "We pretty much had the whole team coming back. Obviously we lost Cedric Benson and Derrick Johnson, but we had the nucleus and the majority of our team coming back. We knew what we were and what we had. We trusted our coaching, and we trusted our development. For us, there was one goal and that was to get back to Pasadena. 'Take Dead Aim' was our motto in the off-season. We were looking long term. We wanted to win a national championship, and we weren't going to let anything get in front of us."

In the off-season Texas defensive coordinator Greg Robinson left to become the head coach at Syracuse. The introduction of new

Texas defensive coordinator Gene Chizik was exciting news for Huff. Chizik's defense featured a prominent role for defensive backs to play creatively and had propelled Auburn defensive back Carlos Rogers to the Jim Thorpe Award, the award given to the nation's top secondary player. The Thorpe Award was a major goal for Huff, and he knew he could win it during his senior season.

"I loved it because he just had a Thorpe winner," Huff said. "Carlos Rogers won the Thorpe the previous year, so I knew the defense was built for the secondary. It was built for defensive backs to make plays. I was happy. That was one thing with his defense—it gave the safeties responsibilities to make plays. It wasn't necessarily freelancing, but if I watched as much film as they do, I could make checks and adjustments to get us in the right defense. For me it was the freedom to use my football IQ and instincts to help the defense out and make plays."

Huff's first step toward the Thorpe was drawing the toughest assignment in every game. As Texas faced dynamic players such as Ohio State's Ted Ginn Jr., Oklahoma's Mark Clayton, and USC's Reggie Bush, Huff usually drew the man-to-man assignment. Checking the opponent's best weapon allowed Chizik to dedicate resources elsewhere when facing high-powered offenses.

"I could run with any of them," Huff said. "Ohio State had Ted Ginn and Santonio Holmes [Jr.]. They'd put me on Ted Ginn and let me have him by myself, and we could lean to Santonio Holmes. Michael Griffin at free safety could lean to the other guys and not have to worry about me. We knew Adrian Peterson was going to run the ball, so we could put me on Mark and put an extra hat in the box. With Reggie, we didn't want to get him matched up on linebackers or other safeties, so we had certain packages where, depending on where he lines up, we could set the defense. If he was in the backfield, we might run quarters, but if he was split out, we might check it to man, and I'd go out and cover him. We were the quarterbacks of the defense back then, and the coordinators would give us that freedom because they knew we studied the game as much as they did. They'd put the defense in the best position to make plays."

Heading into 2005 the Longhorns would need to work tirelessly to reach their goal of a championship. Nobody had to be urged to work in the summer—the team sweated in the weight room and took part in voluntary workouts. In the process, the players built the type of chemistry necessary to win it all.

"Everybody was there," Huff said. "There was no having to beg guys or drag guys to workouts. We had one goal, and we knew if we wanted to beat USC, we have to be the best Texas team we could be. We'd have summer workouts. We'd drive down to San Marcos and scrimmage Texas State in 7-on-7 down there. Coaches probably didn't like it, but we were tired of going against Vince every day. We wanted to go down there and go against someone else. One day a week we'd go down there, and one day a week they'd come up to Austin. Just going against someone else, that was the time we were on the same team rooting for each other. That's something you really can't do until you get into the season. It built that team camaraderie."

Huff had a special season in 2005, capping off a strong career. Huff recorded seven career interceptions and returned four of them for touchdowns, setting a school record. Not a bad stat for a player who dropped so many passes in high school, he earned the derisive nickname of "Huff Hands."

"Between me and Rod Babers, we probably had the worst hands," Huff laughed. "Just imagine if I would have caught all of them—I would have broke the record by far. I definitely dropped more than I caught, and a few of them were on the way to the end zone. The record could have been a lot further out there. Nobody was going to catch a ball on my side, not even me."

During his senior year, the Longhorns faced a tough trip to Columbus, Ohio, to face Ohio State in the Horseshoe. It was one of college football's most storied and hostile environments, but Texas was up for the challenge. Once again, Huff drew special inspiration for the game from his time as a young man watching his hero Charles Woodson play against the hated Buckeyes.

"I remember watching that game every year and seeing Charles Woodson make plays in that game, in that stadium, and on that field," Huff said. "Those are games Texas never plays. Obviously we do now with Alabama coming in, but back then we scheduled cupcakes for the nonconference schedule to get to the conference undefeated. When we saw that on the schedule, we were all excited. Those are the games you want. You want to play in those big games and hostile environments. We played OU at the Cotton Bowl, which was hostile, but it wasn't a home-and-home. Playing Arkansas was probably the rowdiest, loudest environment we had. Ohio State was just a different animal. It was a night game, and that environment just springboarded us for the rest of the season. Everybody hates Texas. We always get their best, even if they've never played Texas. We definitely got the best shot from everybody."

Texas moved through the season mostly without incident. After a scare at the hands of Texas A&M, the Longhorns would face Colorado in the Big 12 Championship Game. Texas made easy work of the Buffaloes, winning 70–3 as the team rounded into shape for the final test of the season.

"Nothing was getting in the way," Huff said. "I feel like we weren't even playing Colorado. We were playing USC that day. We were playing up to a standard, and Colorado just happened to get in the way. Nothing was going to stop us that day."

Now on a collision course with USC, Texas would have to face the national media's overwhelming praise of Southern Cal. The Trojans had won two straight national titles and were aiming for a three-peat. With a wealth of talent on the roster, including what would be two Heisman Trophy winners following Reggie Bush's win that year, Texas heard nothing about themselves and everything about how unbeatable USC was. Their head coach used that to his advantage.

"Mack knew that," Huff said. "He had it on the TV in the locker room. That's the politician in Mack. He knows how to push buttons and get certain guys riled up. Even before we went out to California, we were tired of hearing it. They had a countdown on ESPN about how they were the best team ever. For us it was like, 'If we beat them, does that make us the best team ever?' We were ready to go out there and play."

Before they could get to the game, several Longhorns were up for postseason awards. Huff was part of that group as he found himself a finalist for the Jim Thorpe Award. He would go on to win the first Thorpe Award in Texas history, which would allow him the opportunity to meet his hero.

"I feel like it really didn't hit me until I went to the Thorpe banquet and Charles Woodson was there," Huff said. "That was the first year he ever came back, and that was my first time meeting him. I got his Michigan signed jersey and his Raiders signed jersey at the banquet. For me, it was all surreal. I truly realized what I did. At the award show, we won the award, but we went straight to getting ready for the

national championship. After that you go straight to getting ready for the Combine and pro day. You never get to sit down and think about everything you accomplish until after that year. It's a good problem to have. It wasn't until that moment when I met Charles Woodson at the dinner that it really hit me."

Winning the Thorpe was a great honor for Huff. The award is prominently displayed in a trophy case inside his house today. He was honored to follow in the footsteps of Woodson, but the bigger honor was how the award reflected on the team overall.

"I wanted to win the Heisman too because he won the Heisman," Huff said. "That was probably more out of reach. For me, I was excited that Woodson won it, but, for me, it was more of a team award. I knew I wouldn't have won it if we were a five- or six-win team, even if I had the same stats. It acknowledged we were a top-10 defense, and we were the best team in the country. It was special for the team and the brotherhood we had."

One award the Longhorns didn't take home was the Heisman Trophy. Vince Young fell short to Reggie Bush in a landslide victory for the USC back. Collectively the team was disappointed, but they also knew that Young would be hell on wheels in Pasadena.

"That goes back to being a player-led team," Huff said. "We knew that one of our brothers deserved the award and should have won it. We go up there and see our brother almost ready to cry. We could tell on his face at the ceremony that he was ready to get back to work. The first thing he did was call me and Rod Wright and said, 'It's time to go to work and get the real trophy.' We definitely played with a chip on our shoulder because we knew he was the best player in the country. He should have won it. We knew we were playing for Vince, and we knew we were going to get his best. Any time you pissed Vince off, that's the Vince we wanted to see every week. We knew defensively they were going to make plays, but we had to do our job and get stops and get the ball back. We had faith in our defensive staff and our players that we could make our plays as well."

Just like superheroes in the comic books, Michael Huff had an alter ego. The mild-mannered former track star turned to "Willie Jenkins," his nom de guerre on the field, when he needed to play nasty.

"I think it was my freshman year—I broke up a pass on the sideline against Oklahoma State, and I got up and stepped on the guy's back on the way to the sideline," Huff said. "He's the asshole. I'm more of a quiet and humble, chill guy. Once someone starts talking a little trash, Willie Jenkins would come out. He's the guy Coach Akina would find a way to bring out in the game, because he was the one who was down there in the pit tackling people. He's the opposite of the track guy. We needed Willie on game day, and we needed Michael in the classroom and off the field. He was kind of like my game-day alter ego. Everybody needs an alter ego. That way you can do stuff you don't normally do and just blame it on that."

When Texas arrived in Pasadena, they discovered they were retracing their steps from the previous season. In many ways, the game was just a redux of the previous year. Texas stayed at the same hotel, played on the same sideline, and ate the same meals as they had the previous year in Pasadena.

"We'd been on that stage," Huff said. "We'd been in that stadium on that grass a year ago. For us, it was just the same game but a different opponent. We knew that Michigan was obviously a great team. We knew USC was a great team. It was just another great game and another great environment. It was the same walk up to the stadium. We stayed in the same hotel. Everything was exactly the same."

USC held a 7–0 lead early in the second quarter. The Trojans were marching down the field and threw a screen pass to Bush, who evaded Texas safety Michael Griffin in the open field and set off for the end zone. Bush ran 35 yards as Huff began to close in on him to make the tackle. Not content with what would have been a huge gain, Bush inexplicably tried to lateral the ball to a teammate who had no idea it was coming. Huff recovered the mishandled ball, and Texas would kick a field goal on the ensuing drive. USC's momentum waned following that play, and Texas started to grab their own piece of the momentum pie.

"I still have no idea what he was trying to do," Huff said. "Usually when he breaks away, he scores easily. I don't know if it was just the Texas speed and he didn't expect anyone to be around him. I didn't even see anybody around. I don't know who he was pitching it to. I went back and looked at it on TV and saw someone back there randomly, but I had no idea what he was doing when he threw it. I make fun of Michael Griffin all the time because he was the one Reggie shook early in the play. I tell him if he would have tackled him, we would have never got the ball back. They probably would have went down and scored on that drive, so I always thank him for getting shook."

In the Rose Bowl, Huff recorded 12 tackles. No tackle would be bigger than the final play he made in his college career. Texas trailed by five and faced USC on fourth down with two yards to go. LenDale White ran power from the I-formation at will that day, amassing 124 yards and three touchdowns. With the game on the line, Huff fired into the backfield and stopped White short of the chains.

"We hadn't stopped that play all game," Huff said. "It was just I-formation and power downhill. It's simple football. With Reggie on the sideline, we knew what they were going to do. If they ran a pop pass or something else, I'd be fine losing that way. For us, we were talking in the huddle, and in Cover 3, normally, I'm five or six yards off the line walking down, but at that time I was downhill in the box. The defensive line got a great push and kept their line off of me. I could just shoot the gap, and I got a piece of the guard and fell in there and squirmed my way in. If they would have made that, I knew that was probably going to be my last real play in college football. I wasn't going to go out this way. For me, I gave it all I had. We knew once we got the stop that it was over with. We knew Vince was going to go down and score. At that moment, I ran off the field and took my helmet off. We just knew. Vince is Vince. He was going to find a way. The Heisman snub and all that—he was going to do everything in his power to get in the end zone."

Huff would be named Defensive Player of the Game following his double-digit tackle and fumble recovery performance.

"I didn't even know they gave out Defensive Player of the Game," Huff laughed. "I thought there was just one Player of the Game. If you look at it, I still had my shoulder pads on and all my gear. I didn't expect it. I was on stage with the T-shirt over my pads. I wasn't expecting to go up there and do anything because I didn't know it existed."

Following the game, Huff would go on to prepare for the NFL Draft. He left Texas with 318 tackles, seven interceptions, 44 pass break ups, six forced fumbles and three recoveries. He was selected at No. 7 overall in the 2006 Draft by the Oakland Raiders, where his hero Charles Woodson played his career. Though the league would bring them close, Huff and Woodson never directly crossed paths on the same roster.

"He played his career in Oakland, and the year I got drafted was the year he went to Green Bay," Huff said. "I took the No. 24. The year I left Oakland and went to Baltimore, he came back to Oakland that year and took 24. For like 20 years, the No. 24 went from him to me and back to him."

Following an eight-year NFL career that saw Huff earn All-Pro honors with the Raiders before short stints with the Baltimore Ravens and Denver Broncos, Huff returned to Austin and went to work with Texas head coach Charlie Strong as a volunteer assistant. Now under his third head coach at Texas, Huff transitioned to a role in player development where he can keep in touch with the team and mentor younger players.

"I saw the disconnect from my time up until now between the former players," Huff said. "When I was in college, everyone came back. Everybody was just around. For us, we had a bunch of big brothers there. Even when I was in the league, I would come back. That's why I'm close with Marquise Goodwin. I paid for his family to go to the Olympics when he jumped in London. Guys like Aaron Williams and all them—they were like our little brothers. With the coaching changes, guys come back and don't feel as comfortable. There's been a disconnect between the former players and the program, and the former players built this program. I wanted to be that bridge to the past and the future. I love helping recruiting and getting the right guys in that DB room who fit this brand and fit this legacy and tradition."

Huff's role in player development allows him to give back to his university, stay in touch with the game, and still be a family man to his two children.

"It's all player development now just to be around the guys," Huff said. "I have a nine-year-old and a five-year-old, so it's good. I never wanted to coach. I've had job offers in the Big 12 to be a corners coach or safeties coach. I don't want to do that. You have to be football first, second, and third, and family comes fourth and fifth. Mine has to be football and family. I can still take my kids to school every morning and still pick them up and go to activities."

Huff can be seen at workouts, often in a sleeveless shirt as the once-skinny track kid shows off his NFL physique for everyone to see.

"I go to 6:00 AM workouts," Huff said. "We have the morning practices, so I drop my kids off and head in and be around the guys. I can be done to pick my kids up at 3:00 from school. With technology I'm always a FaceTime away from the guys. They like to FaceTime more than talk anyways, so, for me, it's perfect. I can still be big brother. I can talk to them differently than the coaches can talk to them. I can give them the honest truth and the hard truth. My blood, sweat, and tears are in there. It's part of the gig, and that's why I love it."

Huff is also involved in recruiting from time to time, helping the defensive back coaches with the prospects they are working on. Huff has been aged out for today's teenagers, but he does have another important message to share.

"Now most of these kids weren't even born when [that] Rose Bowl was played," Huff said. "The parents know me more than the kids do. That's the crazy part. I tell them about me and my shoe collection and my shoe store and the businesses I have going on. Now it's more showing them life after football and the business side of it. I played eight years in the NFL, but I was done at 30. Then I had to figure out what's after that."

Huff became involved with several businesses following his playing days. He's part owner of Centre, a fashionable clothing and shoe store with several locations in Texas. He's also involved with

HFactor Water and a gym he runs to promote health and fitness. Living back in Austin, Huff has no complaints about how anything played out.

"For me, it all turned out well," Huff said. "Everything played out perfectly. I wish I'd have run track every year. I ran my junior year, but it wasn't the same taking three years off and putting on 20 pounds. For me, I would have run every year, but that would have cut into spring ball and I might not have developed on the football field. I think it all worked out like it was supposed to."

CHAPTER 9

Rod Babers

Rod Babers grew up in the South Park neighborhood of Houston.

He attended Lamar High School, located just south of the 610 loop that circles the downtown area. Lamar serves as a business magnet school with an international baccalaureate program that invites a wide array of students from the area inside its doors. Lamar's football team boasts notable alumni including Josh Gordon, Brian Orakpo, Brandon LaFell, and Gerome Sapp.

Babers was never the biggest, but he was one of the fastest students in his age group. At 5'8" and 170 pounds, Babers found his way onto the field in high school and started making plays. All-American safety Gerome Sapp was a friend and teammate of Babers, and the group of coaches who came out to see Sapp led to Babers being discovered. With the right eyes on him, Babers performed well and earned the recognition of several schools, including Texas.

"I didn't honestly know I was good enough until I started getting offers," Babers said. "I don't even know if you get letters anymore, but I started to get letters through the high school. That was the big deal. I wasn't getting those letters my junior year. Gerome Sapp played with me in high school. He was the No. 1 safety in the country as a junior and ended up going to Notre Dame. He was my best friend at the time, and we played in the same secondary. Honestly it was a blessing for me that everybody was coming to see my boy Sapp. He played in the NFL and got drafted. He's got Super Bowl rings. Sapp was the real deal. He pushed me because we were going at it. I think I pushed him too, I'd like to say. He's who I worked out with every day. People would come to see Sapp, and they saw us play against Cy-Creek [Cypress Creek High School], who had B.J. Symons, the [future] Texas Tech quarterback. I had a hell of a game. I had two picks, I returned one of them for a touchdown, and had a receiving touchdown. Coach Tim Brewster was there, and he told Mack he had to have Sapp and Rod B. That was the kind of game that really blew me up. That's when I knew I was good enough."

Texas was one of the first schools to show serious interest in Babers, and the early investment paid off. Texas A&M had a strong grip on the greater Houston area, and Babers saw many former and current teammates head to College Station. While he considered the Aggies, the opportunity to forge his own path in Austin was too attractive.

"I had so much love for them, and I was excited about the recruitment of them because they were one of the first," Babers said. "A&M was early on. I'm from Lamar High School. We call it D.B. High now because we produce a lot of good ones. If I'm not mistaken, I don't believe anyone before me in the modern era went to The University of Texas on a scholarship. We had a lot of guys going to A&M and Oklahoma—I remember the pictures being up in the office. There wasn't any from The University of Texas, and I remember that standing out to me. I was thinking I wanted to go to UT. My dad was a big Jerry Gray fan. When Texas came into the picture for me, it was about Texas and Texas A&M, even though my final five was those two, Colorado, Penn State, and Florida State."

Babers was set to graduate in 1999. Florida State was one of the top teams of the decade and showed no signs of slowing down anytime soon. Growing up, Babers idolized Deion Sanders, and the opportunity to follow in his footsteps at Florida State presented itself. As his recruitment heated up, a conversation with Texas A&M head coach R.C. Slocum convinced Babers to stay in the state of Texas, but it ended up backfiring on him as Babers would ultimately head to Austin.

"Florida State probably could have flipped the script," Babers said. "R.C. Slocum is the man. R.C. Slocum had a hell of a pitch, but it was one that blew up in his face. R.C. Slocum, when I told him my five schools, he told me that if I wanted Mom and Dad to come to the games, I shouldn't leave the state. R.C. made me shut off everything outside of the state. That's when I shut off Colorado, Florida State, and Penn State. I had to. I loved Rick Neuheisel at Colorado. That's who was recruiting me up there. We were cool. I was a big fan of Florida State because of Deion Sanders. That's why I wore 21 when I was at Texas. I wanted to be the next Deion Sanders. When I figured out my mom and dad couldn't go to every game, that was it. Texas was in the Big 12, so they could probably go to 9 or 10 games a year. That's all it took for me. At 17 years old, it hadn't clicked to me. I was too selfish, and I wasn't thinking about all of that. R.C. broke it down for me."

Babers saw The University of Texas early on when he was in Austin for a track meet. Tagging along with his All-American teammate Sapp, Babers was able to see a few schools early. When he returned, it would be for an official visit. Texas rolled out the red carpet for Babers and hit the right notes, choosing former Houston-area defensive back Joe Walker to host Babers on the trip. The two knew each other from growing up in the same city and crossing paths several times in high school.

"I want to say Texas Relays was the first time I went up there unofficially," Babers said. "We competed there. We just went to go visit campus, and I don't even know if we talked to football coaches or anything like that. Me and Sapp just wanted to see the university, and at that time, Sapp was big time. I do believe I was just tagging along with him at the time. He had already been on the map. When I went to visit my senior year, Joe Walker was my host. It worked on the official visit, because in Houston I lived down south. Joe Walker was from North Shore. Back in the day—before 7-on-7 and these organized camps—you had to go find work. We'd keep our cleats in the trunk. You would go to different schools and go find work during their workouts. It was like pickup basketball games. We'd go to Welch, we'd go to North Shore, and we'd go to Madison. We'd go wherever. It was when they were just on the verge of having 7-on-7 tournaments, but I met Joe Walker doing that. I also knew him through track. I was a big Joe Walker fan. Back then we didn't have the Internet, so we kept up with guys in the newspapers. I knew who Joe Walker was because he was one of the best defensive backs in the state at North Shore. I wanted to be the best, so I kept up with everyone who was cold in the area. When I ended up going, Joe Walker and Greg Brown were my hosts. That was pretty much all I needed as the intro."

Babers was a recruiting hound who kept up with the other great players in the area as much as one could before the advent of Internet recruiting sites. Using publications such as *Dave Campbell's Texas*

Football and the *Houston Chronicle*, Babers kept tabs on the other top defensive backs in the area.

"I used to keep up with it," Babers said. "I knew all the local guys who were good players. I met a lot of those guys through 7-on-7 when it was in its infancy. We didn't have tournaments—we just had districts that got together at the time. We didn't have the championship that they have today, but we did have some of those competitions. I'd meet them through those workouts because we were just trying to get better. That's why the circuit has blown up now with 7-on-7 and camps. Everybody is trying to do the same thing and find that competition outside of what they usually see at school. You've got to cultivate your craft, and it's really hard to do that when you get into a rut in the off-season."

Tim Brewster led the recruitment for Texas. Brewster is known as a rainmaker on the recruiting trail, and he was the top assistant for Mack Brown before leaving for a stint coaching in the NFL. Brewster left a strong impression on Babers and connected him with other recruits who would turn into lifelong friends.

"Brew makes an impression," Babers said. "He's just got a mouthpiece. I call him the Ric Flair of recruiting. He walks in there swagged out. He might have had gaiters on at the time. There were other people there, but Brew stands out all the time. Me and Brew are still cool to this day. He's the Ric Flair though. He would come in talking trash and telling you everything you want to hear. I can't tell you all the stuff Brew told me—and half of it wasn't true. It was Brew first and my next contact was probably Coach [Everett] Withers. Brew is the one who hooked me up with my boys."

After getting to campus, Babers became inseparable with a few players in his class. The 1999 film *The Wood* told the story of three friends growing up in Inglewood, California. Its popularity at the time led to the friends naming their group after the film and going so far as to get tattoos to immortalize the friendship.

"My boys to this day are the Wood," Babers said. "The Wood is Chris Simms, Bo Scaife, Montrell Flowers, and Kyle Shanahan. The truth is, the core of the Wood is me, Simms, and Scaife. We got linked up before Shanahan came in late, and Montrell was a different class. Me, Bo Scaife, and Simms came in during the '99 class, and we all came in early too. We came in during the summer. There was no scholarship then, so we lived with the players. I lived with Joe Walker back then. We got hooked up because of Tim Brewster. He'd always put us on conference calls together. When Simms committed to Tennessee, Tim Brewster told me not to believe it—he said it from the jump. I didn't have social media, so I wasn't telling anybody, but he was that confident. He used to have us talking together, so that's how I got cool with Scaife. We went down there early and linked up, and Brew is a big part of why that's my crew for life."

The story of Chris Simms and Kyle Shanahan having matching tattoos is popular in today's media and popped up once again this past season, when Shanahan coached the 49ers to the NFC Championship Game. Though it's commonly referenced between the two, the entire group took part in the ritual.

"Once Simms got the tat, everybody had to get the tat," Babers said. "We are brothers. Shanahan was the last one to get it. He told us he didn't know if he was going to, and we told him we were going to have to kick him out of the crew. 'Everybody is getting it, and if you're not getting it, we'd have to kick you out.' They always mention Chris and Kyle's matching tattoos but never the rest, but it's all good. Those are the most famous members of the Wood. For the record, though,

Shanahan got the smallest of the tats. Everyone has slightly different types of tats. Your tattoo is based on your personality. I know people want to make fun of it, but for the record, they aren't matching, and everyone has everyone else's initials on the tat in some way. It's one of those things that I didn't mind it then, but I appreciate it even more now. I'm sure people will talk trash about the crew, but those are my brothers. We wanted to make sure we marked it for life no matter what happens."

Once his recruitment went down the stretch, Babers was really only considering Texas and Texas A&M. Though he ended up taking most of his visits, Babers was leaning heavily toward the Longhorns. A big reason for that was Coach Brown and the trajectory of the program. Coming over from North Carolina, Brown brought a newness to Texas. Brown put together a strong class—most notably landing elite defensive lineman Cory Redding—and Babers felt that Austin was the right place for him.

"I took all my visits," Babers said. "I didn't commit until late. I don't know the exact date, but Cory Redding was already committed and that was a big thing. I had taken my visit to Texas and my visit to A&M. I'd been to Florida State and Colorado. I didn't end up going to Penn State. Once I was able to shut everything down because I wanted to stay in the state, two things really swayed it. At the time The University of Texas was becoming the new 'it' university. Ricky Williams just won the Heisman. They had a young, hip coach in Mack Brown. He's not young now, but back then, Mack coming in was a young, new, hip coach. I remember Mack saying he didn't like Reebok, and he came in and brought Nike. He was a Nike guy coming from North Carolina, but no kids wanted to wear Reebok. Mack knew that, and he was all about relating to young people. Austin and Texas at the time was trending. They were starting to become a lot cooler. Ricky Williams was a big part of that, but when he got Cory Redding and Chris Simms, to me, that just confirmed everything I had been feeling too. Another big part of it was being a Texan and bringing Texas back. I wanted to do that."

On his official visit, Babers was able to see everything about the program. Though that trip is usually a benchmark for recruits, nothing was more important to the Babers family than the in-home visit with Brown. At that time, Texas was still shedding a past of racism and discrimination from the '60s and '70s. The 1969 team was the last all-white group to win a national title. Though Texas had since integrated, the stigma lingered. Babers and his family wanted to see if any of those old feelings were still around.

"Most of it is a blur," Babers said. "Not a lot really stood out from the visit. I had already done my research about Texas. It wasn't really about me going there for the visit. It was more about their in-home visit with me. There were teams that were negative—recruiting against Texas—about the history of Texas being a program that was known for discrimination. They were doing that when I was being recruited. Part of the reason that Sapp didn't end up going to Texas was his mom was not a fan of UT and the history of the school. That still gets thrown out there, but the truth is my mom and dad wanted to see how authentic they were. They wanted him in the house to see how they acted with the family. Once he passes the test, then it's all good. That's what happened to Mack. He drank my mama's sweet tea and sat on the couch. The line that got my mom was when he told her that I would graduate no matter how long it takes. He told her if I go to the NFL that he promised I'd graduate. Strangely enough, the man did keep that promise. I did graduate, and it was Mack that did it.

When I went back to school after I got done playing, I came back to UT, and he asked if I enrolled. He told me to go see Jean Bryant in the academic office. He ended up walking me down there to make sure I went. That's what got Mom sold on Mack. I don't think anyone [else] guaranteed I'd get a degree regardless of what happened. When I went back to school, I didn't know if I could just do that. Everything was paid for. I was back on scholarship once again. Every school doesn't do that, but UT has the funds to do it. I don't know if they use that as a sales pitch, but that should be part of it."

Brown's early success could largely be attributed to the family atmosphere he fostered while at Texas. Babers saw a glimpse of that on his official visit and learned more once he got to campus.

"They accepted us as family," Babers said. "Kwame [Cavil] used to do the same thing with me. Kwame used to keep me after practice. He probably just wanted an errand boy, but he wanted someone to work with. I'd stay after practice with him and do bump-and-run drills and then go play off for a few snaps. A lot of times I think he did it for me, but he also did it for him. Those guys were great at being mentors. They wanted to show us how we should treat the young guys coming in after us. Mack was great at cultivating the family. The truth is, I committed to Sally before I committed to Mack."

As we've seen, the story of the Mack Brown era can't be told without a story or two about Sally Brown. The First Lady of Texas Football was a constant presence. Her involvement with recruits and players backed the family environment Brown wanted at his school.

"I was on the phone, and I was talking to Sally," Babers said. "We were having a conversation about my mom and my girlfriend at the time. I thought we were going to end up getting married or something. I was telling her that I already had visions about the wedding—I was telling her specifics about stuff like that. It was probably a 20-minute conversation that had nothing to do with football or Texas. We were just talking about life and family, and I committed to Sally before I committed to Mack. That was how Mack presented it. She was the First Lady of Texas Football, and she was always concerned with how my mom was. She'd always ask if I'd called my mom and checked in. She was never concerned about football or my injuries. She may have talked to me about class, but they did a great job of making you feel like you were part of a real family, and it started at the top with Sally."

Before Babers committed to The University of Texas, Texas A&M made a strong push for him. The Aggies were coming off of a Big 12 Championship and had a strong, physical defense called the Wrecking Crew. Though Babers found their defense impressive and connected with R.C. Slocum early, College Station just wasn't a desirable destination for him.

"I loved the Wrecking Crew," Babers said. "They had just won the Big 12 and were coming off of a successful season. I thought I vibed with Austin a little bit better than College Station. It turns out I was right because I'm still here. I got advice from somebody who told me that if I was going to a university where you pictured yourself living there in the future, that wouldn't be a bad place to go to school. I knew I was going to one of the two, and Austin seemed like a better place to live than College Station. My parents are from the country, and I'm just not a country boy. There are people who love hunting and riding horses and all kinds of stuff, but I'm a city boy. My mom and dad liked A&M a little bit more than I did, but they liked Mack enough that they knew A&M was a good school, but Austin fit me a little bit better."

When Babers got to Austin, he played for defensive coordinator Carl "Bull" Reese. Reese was an old-school coach who preferred to use the top athletes he had access to at Texas primarily in man coverage. Though it was effective most of the time, the advanced passing offenses developing in the Big 12 were a perfect foil.

"It was bump-and-run man," Babers said. "He was adamant about it. We were so good at it that it worked 90 percent of the time when we played Oklahoma because they ran the Air Raid at the time, and they ran a ton of crossing routes and rub routes. When we'd play Texas Tech, it would come back and bite us too."

Growing up in Houston, Babers never had a great appreciation for the Red River Shootout. While Oklahoma was the historic rival for Texas, he always saw Texas A&M as the more important matchup. While he was at Texas, Babers saw the transformation of the two rivalries as Bob Stoops elevated Oklahoma to a national power.

"I didn't really know anything about the rivalry," Babers said. "When Mack recruited you, Mack made a point saying, 'We've got to beat A&M and Oklahoma.' The A&M rivalry was more top of mind because I knew more guys there. I was close to going to A&M because I had a teammate in high school who went there. I knew about that rivalry because of that. The Texas-OU rivalry—I didn't know how important it was. Mack had to break it down for us, which is why I think we got our butts kicked early in that rivalry until it became part of the DNA of the program that we had to beat Oklahoma. Maybe A&M was a bigger power earlier on because of the Southwest Conference days, but it changed while I was there. A&M wasn't the true threat—it was Oklahoma. That changed as soon as Bob Stoops got there and won the national title."

There is no game like Texas-OU. The annual matchup between the Red River rivals is an emotionally charged matchup between two good teams and usually favors the program that can handle the swings. Early in his career, Babers didn't understand the meaning of the game and neither did many of his teammates.

"It hurt us both of those two years," Babers said. "My first game was '99, and that was the Mike Leach fake dummy script game. He dropped the script on the field. Tom Herman and Oscar Giles, who were graduate assistants at the time, took it up to Bull Reese and he fell for it. We got down 17–0 and had to come all the way back. Luckily we won it. That was my only win as a UT football player against OU. In 2000 we got blown out. We didn't understand the vitriol. We didn't understand the magnitude, even after that wild and crazy game in 1999. After 2000 we understood because Bob Stoops changed the culture at Oklahoma and turned them into a true superpower. Texas had to match it after that. Batman needs a Joker. If not for Bob Stoops, Mack Brown probably never wins a national title. He pushed Mack Brown by winning the national title in his second year. The pressure was on Mack immediately. He had no time to enjoy his recruiting classes or the fact he was good with the boosters and donors. Immediately people started whispering. Mack had to evolve quickly. That's why he started tweaking the staff, and one of the best moves he made was hiring Coach Akina. He made some moves that put him on the right path, but I don't think he would have without being pushed like that by Bob Stoops. It would have been too easy for Mack because it was too easy for a while."

As he played out his career against Oklahoma, Babers learned the game was about riding the waves that each year would present and answering the opponent's momentum.

"That game is about answering," Babers said. "The other team is going to make a play. It's just two great teams going at it. It's about if you will answer if they make that play. It's a heavyweight boxing match. We were just never able to get the momentum enough to win that game. The momentum is so strong, and it can almost turn into a landslide. That's what happened to us in 2000—we never answered. Oklahoma came out and hit us right in the mouth, and we just kept getting hit. That's why coaching is big in that game. You've just got to know that you have to take momentum back now, and that affects your play calling."

Babers was also front and center for a quarterback battle that would split the locker room. Young hotshot Chris Simms came in as the top quarterback in the country and would battle incumbent Major Applewhite. While Simms had the physical talent every coach coveted, he had a penchant for faltering in big moments. On the other hand, Applewhite shone when the lights were the brightest. These controversies force the players to choose sides and can cause rifts within the locker room. That quarterback controversy probably held Texas back from achieving the heights it could have.

"Ultimately a team wants to win, but there's no doubt everyone had an opinion on who could help you win games," Babers said. "Some guys probably thought it was Major, some guys probably thought it was Simms. Also the way some guys are received in the locker room matters. Some of the younger guys had issues with Major and some guys had issues with Chris Simms because of the perceived silver spoon in his mouth. They thought he was given everything and the starting quarterback position. I think everyone had their own idea about which one of those quarterbacks would be best for the culture of the locker room and which one of those guys could help you win games. I'm not sure they were always the best, and I'm not sure it was always the same person. It was tough for Mack Brown because he decided to call the quarterback competition instead of letting it play out. Major probably would have won the quarterback position. He thought Simms gave us a better chance to win and gave us a higher ceiling as a team. I don't know if that was the right call or not, because in big games there was no doubt that my man Simms would under-achieve. It split the locker room. Quarterback competitions always do. It's like an election—when you step in that voting booth, you're voting with your own self-interest. Locker rooms are no different. They are just people. Everybody picks their guy, and I think the way Mack played it was probably ill-advised."

Babers had a strong career on the field, finishing his senior year as a finalist for the Jim Thorpe Award, the honor given to the nation's top defensive back. His contributions on the gridiron helped Texas win big during his time on campus, but he also contributed off the field. Choosing player hosts for official visits is important, and "Rod the Recruiter" helped Texas secure some big talent. Considering the résumés of players he hosted, no win was as big as Derrick Johnson. The All-American linebacker developed into one of the best players in Longhorn history, and Babers contributed to landing him after hosting him on his official trip.

"D.J. was definitely the biggest I had," Babers said. "I had Edorian McCullough back in the day. I didn't get that reputation until D.J. I was always pretty outgoing, but I was told we had to get this guy. I was given the responsibility because everyone liked me. To me, it was easy. I just told him the real. I told him that I was told he was the best defensive player they've ever seen. I told him if he was as good as they say he is, he'd be playing as a freshman, and if he could do that, he'd go to the NFL. It turns out they didn't talk him up enough. There are a lot of guys I've seen in person that are freaks, but he might be in my top 10. He was a mutant. When we saw him out there as a freshman, we knew he was going to be a problem. There was no doubt he had to see the field. Cory Redding was like that too, along with Nathan Vasher."

Babers was also around for the introduction of Vince Young. A Houston high school legend, Young made his mark in Babers' hometown and came to Texas during Babers' senior year. Though he only played scout team as a redshirt player, Young showed Babers glimpses of what he would be in years to come.

"I remember V.Y. from H-Town," Babers said. "Everyone thought he was going to be a basketball star. He definitely would have been hanging out in the crew that I was with, and B.J. [Johnson] and Simms were probably going to be in that crew together with the wideouts. They would have given him to someone they trusted and someone they knew would give him the red-carpet treatment. B.J. Johnson could do that. I knew about V.Y. though. I don't think I was in on that recruitment closely being on the defensive side of the ball, but we knew about V.Y. because the legend and folklore followed him from H-Town. Me being from South Park and him being from Hiram Clarke—that wasn't that far apart. Madison was in our district back in the day. I remember seeing him on the scout team making plays. V.Y. has pretty much been the same even when he wasn't on the national stage in prime time. That swagger and trash talk you'd see—he was the same guy even when he was the quarterback for the scout team. It was only a matter of time. We knew V.Y. was going to be special, we just didn't know how much time it was going to take."

When Babers left after the 2002 season, he knew the team could go on to win a championship. They were close during his time, coming up just short in 2001 and finishing with a disappointing season in 2002. Still the overall roster talent was getting better, and practices were a strong indicator of how talented the team was.

"We should have played for one, so I knew we were close—'01 and '02 we were good enough to at least play in BCS games, and we obviously came up a little short," Babers said. "One of those teams should have been able to beat Oklahoma. We played in the Big 12 title game, and we should have been able to beat Colorado after beating them earlier that year. If we do, we play in the national title game against Miami. I knew we were close and that was from practices. Our practices when I first got there were competitive, but they were nothing like practices were when I left. Our one-on-ones were brutal in a good way. By the time I left, it was me, Nathan Vasher, Michael Huff, Cedric Griffin. We had a lot of young talent at the DB spot, and you had those wide receivers who set the tone—Roy Williams, B.J. Johnson, and Sloan Thomas were still there. Bo Scaife [became] an NFL tight end. The one-on-ones we had—we'd just make each other better. I remember how physical it would get and how contentious it would get. We would go at each other, and the coaches would be cussing each other out. I'd go out there and demand who I'd go up against. That's how we made each other better. Iron sharpens iron, and I think we got to that point at every position. It took us a little bit longer to get there on the lines of scrimmage, but that's when the games are easy. Nobody else had talent like we had. Practices are when you would get better. The games were fun because nobody out there was as good as the guys I was going against every day in practice. If I can lock down Roy Williams in practice, I could go into games almost arrogant."

In the early 2000s Texas was known as DBU, or Defensive Back University. A large part of that was the legacy that players such as Johnnie Johnson and Jerry Gray left. Babers was part of the DBU resurgence at Texas and that came from defensive backs coach Duane Akina who replaced Everett Withers during Babers' career. Throughout the early 2000s, no school produced more talent at the position than the Longhorns who featured two Thorpe Award winners and countless draft picks. Though the current Texas program isn't reaching that standard, Babers takes pride in his part of the legacy.

"To me, I think the title is like a championship belt," Babers said. "It's passed along. Texas can get it again, but you can't claim to be DBU where we are at right now. We were at one time DBU, so once you're a champion, you're always a champion. I think it's in our DNA because we were the original. Coach Akina was a new-age coach who really wanted to break us down mentally and intellectually. As a true teacher, he wanted to find out how we best learned the concepts. Everyone has their own way of processing, and he'd teach us in our own way. He would give us all the tools we needed, but we had to make the right decision. That blew my mind and changed my mind about football. This is why Coach Akina was also great. When he first came in, he was a fan of Texas DBU. He taught us the history about it. My pops was already telling me about Jerry Gray and Johnnie Johnson—Coach Akina came in and started talking about those guys and Noble Doss. He actually started making us appreciate the legacy of DBU. He told us it was part of his plan. He told us we were going to bring back DBU. We may have let Florida State claim it for a while and Ohio State had it at some point, but we were going to bring it back here. We started taking pride in it, and you get what you emphasize. We started watching the best secondaries around the country. We started coming up with our own celebrations because we were going to be celebrating a lot. We needed something that was a signature to us because everyone was going to watch us celebrate across the country. In 2001 we had the top pass-efficiency defense in the country. We were nasty back there. He wanted to boost our football acumen. We started watching film and talking about route combinations. Working with Coach Akina and Shanahan at the time, they were really tight because both are football intellectuals. One of my great lessons in football was talking to Shanahan after practice. Shanahan as a wide receiver—and this is how I knew he was going to be an amazing coach—he started talking about canceling routes. If you're a DB, you should make sure you know the route tree. Once a guy passes six yards, no slant, no hitch, no quick out. Once I get past 15, no curl, no out, and, depending on how strong the quarterback's arm is, you probably aren't getting a comeback. It was an epiphany in my brain that I had to start canceling routes as he's moving toward me. Coach Akina was the one who brought back DBU though, because youngsters weren't appreciating it. I did because of my pops, but young people weren't appreciating it the way Coach Akina made us appreciate it."

After completing his career at Texas, Babers was drafted in the fourth round of the 2003 NFL Draft by the New York Giants. Following a four-year career that saw Babers spend stints with the Giants, Lions, Buccaneers, Broncos, Bears, and Hamilton Tiger-Cats of the CFL, Babers returned to Texas to complete his degree and work toward a career in coaching. While there, he subbed in on a radio show on 1300 AM *The Zone* in Austin and his media career was born.

"I was back and going to school. I was thinking of getting into coaching," Babers said. "Actually I was coaching at St. Michaels

[Academy] at the time. Chip Brown was hosting a radio show at the time in Austin, and the late Sean Adams was going out of town, and Chip asked me to sit in. Me and Chip had a hell of a time. He told me I should do it and it would be good for me. I started doing more subbing in, and I got offered a couple of gigs. Around that time, I was approached by somebody from Texas. I was told to go work for *The Zone* because it was the flagship station. I worked with Craig Way for like eight years over there and learned a lot. I thought it would be a temporary gig—15 years later it is what it is. I've been doing some television stuff, and I've been trying to get back into some writing, but it's crazy. I've been thinking about getting into individual defensive back coaching because I'm passionate about it. I've gotten some offers to get back into coaching again, but I know how much time it takes. Whenever they fire me from this gig and I'm done with media, I'll probably try coaching."

Babers also took a job working as the sideline reporter for the Texas radio play-by-play broadcast. He was able to stay involved with Texas football along with his daily radio show, but a comment he made about the team's football IQ led to a run-in with his former head coach and a decision to ultimately walk away from the play-by-play job. Now on the opposite side of the line, Babers saw how relationships could change with one comment.

"I love Mack. He's the man, and we've since hugged it out. We're good, but we did have a bit of a falling out," Babers said. "I was doing sideline reporting, and Texas was playing badly, which has been all too common in the past 10 years. I had a daily radio show, and Longhorn fans, they don't want to hear you pump sunshine. I was telling it like it is, and I'm sure Mack was listening or at least someone behind the burnt orange curtain was. They didn't like what I was saying, and

Mack called me into the office. I think the comment that upset him was I said something about the team having a low football IQ. That was a comment he brought up several times. He told me he didn't like me talking about his players like that. I apologized because I didn't mean to insult the players, and I appreciated him taking up for them because he would have done the same for me. I told him I had an obligation to an audience of Longhorn fans who want my expertise as a former player, and they wanted authenticity. We agreed to disagree, and essentially Mack didn't want me to quit, but he told me he was disappointed I disrespected the family. Within 24 hours of that meeting, I decided to resign from doing the sideline gig. Mack did not pressure me to resign, but I thought about the postgame interviews being awkward. I didn't want to be a distraction. I decided to resign, and Quan Cosby took over. I just told them I was good and I wanted to focus on my radio show because I had an obligation to that.

The path forward created a brighter future for me, and the sideline gig was too stressful, and I was a distraction to the program. The locker room is a sacred place, and if someone is in there that isn't trustworthy or believed to not be trustworthy, they shouldn't be there. I may have been that person at the time, so I just decided to make everyone's job easier. Me and Mack are good now. That's why I love that dude. He's going to take up for his players. That's family to him, and I was talking bad about his family. Funny enough, when you go to the media, you aren't so much family. When Mack became a member of the media, he started to see how it really was."

These days you can find Babers on the airwaves of 104.9 FM *The Horn* in Austin doing a drive-time radio show with Mike Hardge. Babers also cohosts the weekly podcast *The Longhorn Blitz* with Jeff

Howe of *247Sports*. A budding star in radio, Babers feels that it might never have worked out this way had he not chosen Texas.

"I can't say I have any regrets," Babers said. "I made some dumb decisions, but I learned from all of them, and I'm still here. As a 17-year-old I think I made the right decision. Choosing Texas was definitely the right choice. I'm not sure how I came to the conclusion. It could have been hot women or the city was better. I'm not sure how 17-year-old Rod B. did it, but 17-year-old Rod B. made the right choice. If I wasn't a Longhorn today, I'm not sure how this life would [have turned] out."

CHAPTER 10

Aaron Williams

Confidence is a hallmark of Aaron Williams' game.

The athletic defensive back was one of the best to come through Austin, and he played with an incredibly high level of confidence and swagger. That confidence was well earned—Williams came from an athletic family. His father, Anthony Williams, played at the college level and his uncle Ken Taylor won a Super Bowl with the 1985 Chicago Bears.

Williams was active in athletics from a young age. Born in San Jose, California, Williams and his family moved to the Austin suburb of Round Rock when he was 11 years old. Williams was active in youth football, baseball, and track, but when he got to middle school, he started to get an inkling he had a future on the gridiron. As he moved into high school, he consistently put himself in situations to compete against the best in the country in order to test himself.

"When I was in middle school, I just knew I was better than everybody in my city," Williams said. "So if I was better than everybody there, I had a good enough chance to compete with the people in the state. We have the best athletes in Texas, whether it be basketball, baseball, or football. You're already competing with the top guys, so I just realized if I could compete with guys in Texas, I could compete with anybody in the country. I was supposed to play on varsity my sophomore year, but I had transferred, so they ruled me ineligible. When I was dominating my sophomore year in practice against the varsity guys who were a few years older than me, I knew I had a bright future. I went to the All-American Combine in San Antonio, and that's when guys from all over the country come through. I competed, and I went against the best. I was not afraid. I didn't care how many stars a guy had, I just loved competing. I loved the competition. When I went out there and I held my own, I knew I could do this."

That national Combine kick-started Williams' recruitment and lit the fuse that would explode during his junior season at Round Rock's McNeil High School. Though he was zoned to attend Round Rock Stony Point High School, a decision to attend McNeil for their high school engineering program caused him to be ruled ineligible by the University Interscholastic League, which serves as the governing body for Texas high school sports. Once he really got on the field at the varsity level, schools started showing up.

"I wasn't even supposed to be at that camp," Williams said. "I didn't even get invited until the night before the camp was supposed to happen. I think my dad had signed me up or made a call to see if they could squeeze me in somehow. Right before I was going to bed, he told me I wasn't going to school, I was going to San Antonio, and he told me I had a huge opportunity to show my talent. I went and dominated and did a really good job."

Baylor was the first school to show interest, but soon other coaches would come. Texas coaches Mack Brown and Duane Akina made the short drive over to McNeil to see him as a junior. McNeil isn't considered a prospect factory by any means—the school excels more on the academic side—but Williams' talent allowed the spotlight to shine on his teammates.

"I think it was right after that Combine," Williams said. "I remember the very first letter I got was from Baylor. I was excited. Nothing against Baylor, but they just weren't who they are today. At the same time, I was excited to get interest. After a couple of games, the letters started coming in super heavy from every school. Coaches even came to my practice, which was really cool. I don't think I would have had the same experience had I stayed in California. My school wasn't even that good, but I had Mack Brown come to the high school along with Duane Akina. TCU, Baylor, Texas Tech—I had a lot of coaches come to the school for me, and that was so cool. Not only was it cool for me, but I thought it was cool for my teammates too. There were some guys on the team who really had the talent, but they didn't have the support system I had. My dad was throwing my name out there left and right trying to get me opportunities to get some type of look. For the coaches to come out to see me and see my teammates, I thought that was pretty cool too."

Williams felt destined to end up at Texas. A chance meeting in middle school with Texas strength coach Jeff Madden's son led to an outing that would set his future on a path to burnt orange.

"It's weird how everything lines up," Williams said. "When I first got here, I went to Ridgeview Middle School. Jeff Madden, the old strength and conditioning coach at UT, his son went to my middle school and we became really good friends. One day he asked me if I wanted to go to his dad's job. I didn't know what his dad did at the time, and he told me he was the strength coach at UT. We went to a game. I'm not really big into live games, but I got the whole experience. I got to go in the weight room. I got to go in the locker room and meet Vince Young, Roy Williams, and Cedric Benson. I got to meet a whole bunch of these Texas legends. I was hooked. The way they take care of their recruits at that time—they showed you so much love. We were winning, and we were a prestigious school. Just that tour and being in the locker room and having the current players be cool with me without even knowing me was really cool. Coach Brown was so cool to me, and I was just this little 12-year-old kid. I kid you not—I came in and introduced myself, and I told him I'd be the next player he'd recruit in the next six or seven years. I got invited to the Texas junior day camp and did a phenomenal job there, and they told me they wanted me there."

Once Williams was officially on the radar as a junior, it didn't take long for Texas to reel him in. After visiting Austin for their customary Junior Day event held in the early spring to kick off the following cycle, Williams was offered by Texas head coach Mack Brown. Though he wouldn't announce his intentions until later in the year, Williams made his commitment at that moment.

"That's all they had to say," Williams said. "I didn't really care about any other school. There was no other school in my mind. Texas was my school, it was my home, and it was down the street from where I lived. How could I beat that? We did a tour and then Coach Brown would invite every player to his office. I'm sure not everybody had the same discussion, but we went in there to his office that looked like a presidential suite at the Ritz-Carlton. We sat down, and I was nervous. I thought it was really cool, but I didn't know why me and my parents were in there with the head coach. It was a three-minute conversation, and he officially made the offer. I saw my mom cry so hard, and I felt like I made it. I was only a junior, but I knew I'd made it to where I was destined to go. From there on out, I just wanted to have fun with it."

The meeting with Brown and other Texas players as an adolescent was written on his brain with indelible ink. Williams huddled with his family after speaking with Brown and decided to give the Longhorns his commitment.

"I committed on the spot," Williams said. "I'm not going to say they groomed me to liking UT, but they had early access to me. They already had a relationship to me prior to Junior Day. They knew who I was, but they knew me as a little kid. They had never seen me in action like that. When they finally did, they went ahead and made the offer. My dad told me that if that was what I really wanted to do and where I wanted to be, I should commit. But he told me that if I commit, this was where I was going. There is no decommitting and going somewhere else. If I told somebody I was going to do something, I had to be a man of my word and follow through. I probably thought about it for 30 or 35 minutes, but I didn't really know why I was thinking about it. I did it right there. I remember Coach Brown asked me to keep it quiet for a long time because it was so early in the process of recruiting. I couldn't really tell anyone but my girlfriend at the time."

For kids who grow up in Austin, The University of Texas is the top team. While those who grow up in Dallas or Houston might idolize the Cowboys or Texans, Williams paid attention to what was going on at Darrell K Royal-Texas Memorial Stadium. During his youth, Texas was ascending as the top place for defensive backs to play. Williams saw the greats, including Quentin Jammer and Nathan Vasher, but it was Texas' first Thorpe Award winner, Michael Huff, who really captured his attention.

"The very first guys I looked up to were Nathan Vasher and Quentin Jammer," Williams said. "Quentin was ahead of his time in my opinion. The way he covered and the way he played—he could do everything. When Huff came along, he was the guy I watched highlights of before every game. I just liked the way he played. He wasn't like some big hard hitter or anything, but his game was more precise and more technical. I knew he was just always around the ball. Just by watching him, I could tell he was more smart than just relying on his athletic ability. He knew the game, and he knew how to be in the right position. I was studying him even though I didn't play safety at the time. I think he played corner his freshman year or something, but I tried to imitate everything he did. He was a hero for me, and I finally got to meet him. We just clicked. Ever since then he calls me little bro and that's big bro. He's been taking care of me ever since then. That's seriously family to me. It goes beyond him just being a role model to me."

Nobody was better at recruiting and building his culture in a program than Brown. The Texas head coach preached family and success off the field, and Williams bought in fully.

"He had his own system, and his system worked," Williams said. "It wasn't a strenuous system or very strict. He told us that we had a way of doing things, and we would either get with it or they would find someone that would. Texas had no problem getting the top guys at that time. He didn't force anything on you or make you feel like less of a man. He didn't want to belittle anybody. I may have seen Coach Brown scream three times in my three years at UT. He didn't have to. He had Duane Akina and Will Muschamp screaming at the top of their lungs. He's the head honcho. He was the head guy, but he trusted the guys underneath him to do what they needed to do to get their players ready. He never interfered. Coach Brown never came to a defensive meeting to cut those guys off. The only time he really came in was when he wanted to get everybody on the same page. He made everyone feel welcome and feel like a member of his own family. We were all his sons. There's a reason why he's been as successful as he is."

Another important factor for Williams was his relationship with Texas defensive back coach Duane Akina. Originally born in Hawaii, Akina had a successful playing career as a quarterback at Washington. He transitioned to coach the defensive side of the ball when he was done playing and came to Austin from Arizona after helping to build the vaunted Desert Swarm defense. Where Brown preached family, Akina lived it with his charges. The architect of DBU was like another father for Williams.

"Me and Coach Akina have an amazing relationship," Williams said. "We've gotten into it—it's just part of it when emotions boil up and guys are competing. That's like my third dad right there though. He has his players' back. He don't care if it's the head coach—we were his kids. We represented him, and if we played good, we made him look good. He didn't want anyone messing with him or change his way of teaching. He's a very intense guy and very passionate. He's very honest and very straightforward. He was also very lovable. He brought us to his house. We had cookouts, and we'd always support each other. If we had one or two guys in the draft or the Combine, we'd gather together and support them. He really built a fraternity. It was DBU before I got there, but it was the beginning stage. It was a real tight-knit group, and Coach Akina made it that way. We have to see each other every day, so why not get well acquainted with each other? We communicated. He understood each player was different and every player reacts to coaching differently. He was just very aware of how everybody was, personality-wise."

Late in his recruitment, Auburn threatened to pull Williams away from his commitment to Texas. The Tigers had a fast and physical defense coached by a fiery young assistant named Will Muschamp. When the season ended, Brown made a splash move bringing Muschamp to Austin to run his defense, and Williams was able to get everything he wanted and stay home.

"Auburn was one of the closest teams to make me reconsider going to Texas," Williams said. "The only reason why I didn't go to Auburn was because Will Muschamp decided to come to Texas. That was the reason I was going to go to Auburn. I liked his intensity, and I liked the way he presented himself. I know he wanted to win, I know he wanted to work hard, and I know he wanted to compete. When I heard he was coming to Texas as the DC, I knew I was good and I didn't have to go anywhere. When I saw he was hired on the news, that was it for me."

There are few coaches with the reputation of Muschamp. He was known as "Coach Boom" thanks to a viral video of Muschamp exploding on a sideline in celebration while at Auburn. Williams got a firsthand look at how authentic Muschamp's fire was.

"He cussed out Brian Orakpo on the first day I was there," Williams said. "I'm not going to say they got into it, but Rak made it clear that he wasn't going to talk to him like that because he was a man just like Muschamp was. You don't see players talk to coaches like that. You realize why, because Brian Orakpo was an All-American and first-round draft pick. He does his job, and he doesn't cause any trouble. It made me understand that this is a different ballgame. This isn't high school where coaches can talk to you however and you just have to take it. There's a respect value to it now. We're grown adults, but Will Muschamp didn't care as long as you get the message and you don't get in your feelings and make it personal. At the end of the day, we all wanted to win and all wanted to be great. Coach Muschamp is going to push you though. He's going to push you past your limits. That's one thing that made our team good. He pushed guys further than where they thought they could be pushed."

Muschamp always loomed as a terrifying authority figure known for exploding on his players in moments of frustration. Though it was harsh, Williams never felt it crossed the line. Williams felt the worst the thing that could happen to a player was for Muschamp to ignore him.

"It never was really overboard," Williams said. "He yelled and stuff, but he only maybe punched the whiteboard three or four times. In practice he wasn't doing that, but in meetings, we'd go to the film and he'd get animated. We knew he was just a very passionate and intense person. That's just who he is as a man. We aren't going to fault someone for being themselves. If he didn't get in your ass, you should be worried. You should start thinking about the next college you were going to be at, because it wasn't going to be at Texas. If he's not yelling, he doesn't care about you—you don't mean anything to his game plan. He wanted you to be great in life, but in between those white lines, that didn't matter to him. He had a job, and we had to do our job or he got fired. I didn't think like that at the time, but looking back, I can completely understand why."

Williams hit campus on a mission to make an impact. He showed his stuff early on in off-season workouts, where the seniors on the team took notice. Now one of the guys, Williams was officially part of the DBU fraternity.

"I knew I was playing from the get-go," Williams said. "I knew I wasn't going to get significant playing time. I knew my role was going to be more of a special teams player, which I was fine with because I was playing in front of 100,000 people every Saturday. I had a chance to get my name called in that stadium. I knew I was going to have playing time. I didn't know I'd have that much playing time when Ryan Palmer got hurt against OU. That was an eye-opener for me. When we would do workouts in the summer or 7-on-7 with Texas State, the older guys would always come over and tell me to keep it up. Whenever I got compliments from guys who have been playing this game for a minute, I knew I was ready. Before I even got to campus, Earl Thomas allowed me to sleep in his dorm for a little bit. I would go up there and hang out and work out and just be around the guys. He didn't have much—all he had was his bed and a couch bed, and I was all right with sleeping on a couch bed. The fact that he was willing to allow me to come in his life and take me under his wing was cool. He wasn't even Earl Thomas back then—he was a freshman redshirt with a bright future. During that off-season I figured out how good he was. We had talks. He told me what to expect and what our goals were. We were a tight brotherhood. If you saw Earl or Blake [Gideon] or Chykie [Brown] or Curtis [Brown], you probably saw me."

Williams appeared in 13 games as a freshman and started in 1. As a regular member of the special teams unit, Williams blocked four punts, placing himself atop the school record list. An injury to veteran cornerback Ryan Palmer forced Williams into action in the biggest game of the season. The Texas-OU rivalry is unparalleled in college football, and Williams was in for a culture shock the first time he took the field at the Cotton Bowl.

"My first time there was as a player," Williams said. "I never had any interest in going to the game as a recruit. I always heard about it. You'd see it on TV, and to me it just looked like another game. When you actually get there, it's like the intensity is magnified. When the buses come in, you come in through the fair. You come in through all the people, and fans are fighting before we even walk into the locker room. The tunnel is shared by both locker rooms, so when you come out, you're looking at them. There have been so many arguments and fights in that tunnel—I'm glad I was a part of it. Just having those battle stories is awesome. It really gets intense in that tunnel. The best way I can describe it is you're about to jump out of a plane, and you're looking down with a nervous feeling. That feeling is the exact feeling I had when I found out I was going to go in and start the second half of the OU game. At that time, I focused on my position and my position only. There were only a few plays I paid attention to because I was only in on those packages. When I found out I was going to be starting the second half, Ryan pulled me aside and told me it was just another game. They were stacked. I knew I had to show up. For all players, once you get that first contact out of the way, you're good. You have to get those butterflies out of your system. It was super cool to be a part of that and make an impact in the game."

The 2008 Texas team looked like a team of destiny. That destiny was put on hold when Texas lost a heartbreaker to Texas Tech in Lubbock. Williams' teammate and freshman safety Blake Gideon dropped an interception late in the game that would have iced it for the Longhorns. Threats and harsh words poured in via social media, and the team bond grew even tighter.

"When that game ended, we knew we blew our season," Williams said. "We still had A&M coming up. We were all pissed, but we knew we had to finish the season. We definitely couldn't lose to A&M because that was a big game for us too. We were upset, but I think it lit a fire in us to stick together because everybody outside of the locker room did not like us. All of us had emails and Facebook messages. Twitter was just getting going, and I had messages on there. I had to stay with Blake for a little bit that night because Blake was already fired up. He was ready to fight anyone and everyone, and I wasn't going to allow him to go out there and fight. If he was getting into it, I was going to be into it. We just told Blake it could have been any of us. We told him we had his back and he was a great player. It was just a mistake. We kept tight and you have to with adversity like that. You just have to stick together and finish the mission."

Texas finished the 2008 season just outside of the national title as Oklahoma got the nod to face Florida. Still feeling bitter from the memories of the Texas Tech loss, Williams and the team knew they would have beat Florida and won it all.

"I still believe it to this day," Williams said. "I had several Florida players with me in Buffalo, and I always told them they were lucky we didn't play them in 2008. We felt like we could have had that."

Texas faced a stiff challenge against a talented Ohio State team in the Fiesta Bowl. Williams became a regular contributor on the defense and helped the Longhorns bring home a big BCS win.

"That game was amazing because it was my first time being at a BCS bowl game," Williams said. "I'm pretty sure we were the underdogs, if I'm not mistaken. Going into it, we didn't care. We finished five teams in the top 15. I don't think any other school at that time could have done that. We knew they had guys like Terrelle Pryor and Beanie Wells, but we were just ready. It was a great game. The way it ended—it was probably the second loudest I've ever heard a stadium. After that game, the guys who were coming back on defense, we all had a conversation. We knew this needed to be us in the natty the next year. We told each other we'd do whatever it took to get there. That off-season going into 2009, we knew we had it. We were so in sync as a program."

Heading into the off-season, there was only one goal for the players returning to the roster in 2009.

"It was natty or bust," Williams said. "There was no thoughts of how can we get there. We knew nobody was going to beat us."

The Longhorns navigated through the season unscathed. Set to reach their destiny with only a 9–3 Nebraska team in the way, Texas fans booked their tickets to Pasadena. The Cornhuskers showed up at the Big 12 Championship Game hell-bent on playing spoiler. Behind a dominant performance by Nebraska defensive tackle Ndamukong Suh, the Cornhuskers harassed the Texas offense, holding them to the lowest scoring output of the season. Suh collected 12 tackles and 4.5 sacks as the Huskers almost pulled off the upset. A last-second field goal ended a nail-biter of a game in favor of the Longhorns, but Williams never worried.

"We were calm," Williams said. "At least on the defensive side of the ball we were. Nebraska was not going to score on our defense. We knew going into the game, as long as we did our job, we'd win the game. Even if our offense had a bad game, which they did, we were still good enough to be in the game. That's a scary thought. We could play as bad as possible, and we knew we'd still be in the game. Imagine if everyone was on point. That game would have not even been entertaining. We knew that the offense was struggling, and we never had a guy from the defensive group be critical of the offense. That wasn't our job. We do our job, which is to stop the offense. As long as they don't score, we can win."

Texas went to Pasadena set to win another Rose Bowl and a second national championship in four years. They'd have to take on Nick Saban's burgeoning Alabama program that was set to ignite a dynasty. Texas moved the ball easily on the first drive until Longhorn quarterback Colt McCoy was injured on a quarterback sneak, knocking him out of the game. True freshman quarterback Garrett Gilbert was forced into action, and the Texas defense was in the spotlight. The Longhorns couldn't hold up against the physical rushing attack of Alabama and Heisman Trophy winner Mark Ingram Jr.

"We were like, 'Oh shit,'" Williams said. "Plain and simple that's how we felt. We had a freshman quarterback coming in to try and win a national championship. We got the defense together, and we knew we had to cause turnovers to win the game. We couldn't let them march down the field and burn the clock. I feel like we did a good enough job to keep us in the game. Garrett did a hell of a job for someone who didn't get many snaps in practice and prepare the way that he should have been prepared for a national title game. My hat is off to Garrett because he was put into the fire. Sherrod [Harris] had some experience. It's a bigger game, but he wasn't just coming off a high school season. We were putting in a guy who had just been playing Southlake Carroll to now Alabama. That's two different levels completely. When we saw Garrett manage the game, we knew he wasn't throwing it away. We just had to stop them, but their run game was just too good. They had Trent Richardson and Mark Ingram. Looking back, we were so worried about Julio Jones and their tight end, we felt we could handle the run game. When Trent started busting through and Mark Ingram was marching down the field, we knew it was going to be a hard-nosed, downhill game."

The Texas program never recovered from the loss. Brown was heartbroken following the game and went about changing the program so that they didn't have to rely on one player like they had on McCoy. Texas had been one of the most wide-open and highest-scoring offenses in the last decade, but a switch to a pro-style offense had disastrous results in 2010, as the Longhorns fell to 5–7 just one year after playing for the championship.

"We changed our system," Williams said. "We've had this conversation with a lot of guys. We tried to become Alabama, and that just wasn't our game. We had different skill sets than them. We had a quarterback that could sling the ball, and we didn't have to focus on our run game. That next year Mack wanted to use that blueprint and wanted to get back to the championship doing that. When we got out of the gun, we were like, 'What are we doing?' Garrett Gilbert came from Lake Travis, which threw the ball every play. We were using an NFL playbook under center and downhill. We had never been under center. We were Texas, and we threw the ball. We got out of our own system and tried to use somebody else's blueprint that worked against us."

Williams had a strong career at Texas, posting 106 tackles, three sacks, 12 tackles for loss, 4 interceptions, 24 pass breakups, 6 forced fumbles, and 5 blocked punts. Despite the disappointing season, Williams was ready to return for his senior season. The only thing that could stop him would be a first-round draft grade from the NFL Advisory Board. Williams received the report he wanted before the last game of the season and made the decision to leave school early.

"I had a goal in mind," Williams said. "You can request feedback from the NFL Advisory Board. They will give you a report of where you would land. I told myself I wasn't leaving UT if I got anything other than a first-round grade. I got the report back a week before the A&M game. We weren't going to a bowl, so I wanted to finish the season and get my stats and go on to live my dream. After that A&M game, I remember walking back to the locker room, and me and my parents left the stadium. We all stopped and looked back at DKR and I said, 'I had fun here.' That was it for me. It's funny now—I got so mad at Vince when I was growing up for leaving early. We had just won it all, and he could have come back and won again. When you get into the system, you can see why he left. The opportunity to make millions for your family was great."

Though his parents didn't agree off the bat, they knew the opportunity to make millions was too good to pass up. Williams promised his mother he would return to school after his playing days to complete a degree.

"I promised my mom if I was going to leave early, I'd come back to school and get my degree," Williams said. "If I wasn't going to get my degree, they were really going to try to persuade me to finish, but my dad knew I had a chance to be in the NFL. School wasn't going anywhere."

Williams ended up keeping that promise. He graduated last spring with a degree in education and a minor in communications. More than that, Williams was now eligible for a T-Ring, the tradition started by Darrell K Royal that awarded a special ring to all Longhorn athletes who earn their degree. For Williams, the jewelry is special, but the meaning is even better.

"I'm excited because when you're in a room full of people that have a lot of success, you start to feel some type of way when you don't have those things," Williams said. "Especially when there's no excuse for you not to have those things. They came from where you came from, so there's no excuse. Being out of school for 10 years and coming back was a totally different ballgame. When I went back to school, everything was virtual. It took a lot of discipline and will to really stay focused and not have my ego tell me I was good for life. No matter how much money you have, you need that degree to excel further on than where you want to be. Even though I played in the NFL and had millions, I still felt out of place, like that black sheep in the group. I didn't like that feeling to see others get their T-Ring and have their own businesses. That pushes you. You don't want to be the only one that wasn't successful and didn't achieve things that the others with you did. Plus I promised my mom, so I had to follow through."

Williams was drafted by the Buffalo Bills in the second round with the 34th overall pick. The kid who grew up in sunny California and Austin, Texas, was now headed to western New York. As a 20-year-old headed to a small NFL market, Williams was miserable. It wasn't until he grew up and embraced the community and their rabid "Bills Mafia" fanbase did he realize that Buffalo was exactly where he needed to be.

"Where the hell am I at?" Williams said. "I landed in Buffalo and saw the most industrial, gloomy city. It looked like it hadn't been updated since 1998. I was from California and raised in Texas. Being a Texas guy, we eat, breathe, and sleep Texas. My first two years were terrible. The only reason why was because I didn't give the city a chance. I closed everything off. I was 20 years old. I'd never really left Texas or my parents. I was in New York in an unknown territory, and I hated it because it wasn't Texas. I had a good year. It wasn't like the fans loved me or anything, but they felt I was a solid draft pick. My second year was terrible. The city saw me grow into a man. I introduced myself when I was 20, and I left when I was 27. They saw me go from saying the city was boring to embracing the city. I interacted with them, but nobody recognized me when I was out. It was when I really started playing well and got involved with the community. Here's what I give props to about Buffalo fans—I talked crazy about them when I first got there, and they still embraced me. That's what people don't understand—Buffalo accepts everyone. Once I gave the city a chance and locked in more, it changed. I started maturing. I let my ego go. I thought the NFL life would be about glamour, but it's actually a good thing I didn't go to somewhere like Dallas or the Giants, in a big market. I'm actually fortunate and blessed that I got to go to a very humble and hardworking blue-collar city. If I had went anywhere else, I'd have been caught up in the limelight and never made it."

Williams played for six seasons in Buffalo, totaling 257 tackles and seven interceptions. In 2014 Williams signed a four-year $26 million extension as his career looked to be taking off. One year into the deal, Williams suffered a neck injury that would eventually end his career. He returned in 2016 and scored a touchdown on a blocked field-goal attempt, but his neck issues recurred after a hit against the Miami Dolphins. Williams would never play another game, and he left Buffalo just as the Bills started to develop into one of the best clubs in the NFL. Williams is happy for his old teammates, but watching the game is just too painful now.

"I'm still cool with those guys on the team, but, for me, it's not very pleasurable watching the game of football," Williams said. "I don't really watch it, and if I do, it's just the highlights. Because of the way things ended, it's like watching your ex-wife make out with another guy right in front of you. I worked so hard to be a part of that, and the year I left, they made the playoffs. I was super happy for them, but I was hurting because I didn't feel like I did enough to give the city what they deserved. I was selfishly mad that I wasn't a part of it. I don't watch football at all anymore. Even when I go to UT games, I show up for the pregame and maybe a few minutes of the first quarter. I usually just leave because I don't want to be in the way. I had my time, and I had my glory. I appreciate it, but I don't want to draw focus from the guys there now. I say hi to the people I know there, and I'll speak to the team when they ask me to. When it's game day, I let those guys focus."

Now back in Austin, Williams spends some time around the current team and the Texas campus. His former teammate and good friend Blake Gideon returned to Austin in 2021 as an assistant on Steve Sarkisian's staff. Williams is always available to check in on his friend and speak some motivational words to the team.

"I always reach out when I'm around," Williams said. "I remember I was so excited when Blake got hired because I knew what he gave to this program as a player. Now I'll hit him up and ask if it's cool if I come in and he says I don't have to ask. I show respect to them. Coach Sarkisian has done a great job of welcoming me back to the program and allowing me to come in and talk and just hang out. I love going back to talk to the players because I want them to win like I won. I want them to learn from the mistakes I made."

Now fully retired, educated, and financially set, Williams is still figuring out what he wants to do with life. While he gets out on the golf course regularly and travels as much as possible, the COVID-19 pandemic has limited his ability to travel to places such as Toronto, which Williams counts as his favorite city. Williams also works with local kids to help train them and hone their skills as defensive backs. As he ponders his future, Williams is looking to get back into football with a role in player development.

"I play golf mostly," Williams said. "I'm still trying to find my second passion. I want a hobby that I love that can keep me busy. Right now I'm just mentoring kids. I train defensive backs in the off-season and watch film with them during the season. It's that and travel. Honestly I'm just living life. I've been through so much that I'm okay with saying I deserve to not do anything. As long as I'm giving back in that process, I'm good with where I'm at. My next goal is to get into the player development role at some university or NFL organization. I've been through a lot. I've been from the bottom to the top, and I know what it feels like after you've stopped playing or to be the new kid. I have so much knowledge about how to be successful, why not pass that knowledge on?"

Hindsight is a beneficial view when one can look at their life through the lens of experience and benefit from learning from their mistakes. Williams knows he wouldn't be where he is now without the decisions he's made, but he would change a few small things.

"I'm not going to say regret, because what I did got me to where I am right now," Williams said. "There are not really any regrets, but I would absolutely change a few things. I would take my official visits to every university that wanted me. I encourage every athlete to take every visit they have because it's a free trip. I was so caught up in Texas I just didn't think of anything else. I'd also probably change my focus going into the league and not being worried about being some glamorous superstar everyone knew. I was so focused on the off-the-field stuff, it affected my focus on the field. When I finally recognized that, I thought I was about to get cut. I'd focus more on being a really good football player rather than trying to live the NFL life society portrays."

CHAPTER 11

Bijan Robinson

If Texas is to return to championship form, they will need more players like Bijan Robinson. The junior running back is a one-of-a-kind player capable of jaw-dropping ability from the backfield. He's been no less than a national sensation since arriving in Austin, and he's the best present Tom Herman III left with the program following his tumultuous tenure as head coach.

To trace Robinson's road to Austin, we must go back to his freshman year at Salpointe Catholic High School in Tucson, Arizona. It was there where he first flashed his ability, running 378 yards for four touchdowns on 42 carries. He also added 12 receptions for 233 yards and two touchdowns receiving. Blair Angulo covers the Mountain region for *247Sports*, with his territory consisting of Arizona, Utah, Nevada, and the Pacific Islands. Angulo recalls the first time he saw Robinson in action.

"It was the Pylon 7-on-7 tournament in Mesquite [Nevada] the winter after his freshman season," Angulo said. "He was still a freshman at the time, and I went out to go see his team at Tucson Turf. They had a player by the name of Jamarye Joiner who ended up going to Arizona. He was a dual-threat quarterback and a four-star receiver and a really good player. I was kind of struck by just how dynamic this little running back [Robinson] was for that team. I ended up going up to him and asking who he was, and it all started to click. This was the kid who has been putting up huge numbers and doing really good stuff over at Salpointe Catholic, which is the powerhouse in Tucson. The offers started to roll in. I just saw him running routes and catching the football and looking super explosive in that passing league setting. It was a heck of a first impression."

Recruiting started soon after, with four Pac-12 schools joining the fray. In-state schools Arizona and Arizona State jumped onboard quickly, followed by Utah and Washington. Robinson always showed great maturity as a recruit and never got ahead of himself.

"It's been a blessing to get the attention from coaches and build up some of the options that I've got on the table," Robinson told *247Sports*. "At first it was hectic, and I don't think you can really get used to it, but I've been able to understand the process a bit more and make sure I'm asking all the right questions. I'm hoping to take some more visits in the next few months and then hopefully know where I want to go by the end of summer heading into the season."

Robinson's freshman year put him on the map, and he put together one of the best careers in high school sports history. It started during his sophomore season, when Robinson ran for 2,023 yards and 26 touchdowns on 10.7 yards per carry. Now officially a national recruit, offers started to pour in. Alabama, Oklahoma, Michigan, UCLA, Ohio State, USC, Notre Dame, and many others flocked to Tucson to see what the future five-star running back could do.

At first the West Coast looked like it would be home. Robinson's grandfather Cleo had him watching footage of USC running back Reggie Bush at a young age. Robinson wears the No. 5 in deference to Bush, who captivated audiences during his time with the Trojans. It was for that reason that many thought Robinson could end up at USC. Though the Trojans remained in the recruitment mix throughout his time in high school, questions about the stability of head coach Clay Helton's job always kept them on the outside.

"He's a big-time USC fan," Angulo said. "His grandparents were USC fans. I think he comes from a USC family. He's got a lot of family in Los Angeles, and he grew up idolizing Reggie Bush, as many recruits do or did. They are getting younger and younger, so it's harder to justify them being lifelong Reggie Bush fans, but I think he was the last of the wave of Reggie Bush aficionados. That's why he wears the No. 5. For the longest time, we always heard that he would be playing his college football in Los Angeles. USC wasn't doing that well, and there were a lot of concerns there about the stability of that program, so that also sparked some interest in UCLA, which had just landed Chip Kelly to be the head coach. I think he was just super intrigued about the opportunity to be a running back in that blur, up-tempo, fast-paced offense that Chip Kelly became famous for at Oregon. If you remember, there were so many dynamic running backs in Eugene, like Kenjon Barner, LaMichael James, Jonathan Stewart, and guys like that who were putting up ridiculous stats. He looked at that and thought if he was going to L.A., it could be at UCLA. He told me a couple of times that's where he was leaning. He really liked DeShaun Foster, the former Carolina Panthers running back and former All-Pac-10 running back at UCLA who was the position coach there. Obviously his conversations with Chip Kelly were pretty productive. I think he liked the academic appeal of both schools as well. Bijan is as savvy as there is, even dating back to being a sophomore in high school. I think he realizes what he wants to do in life, and he can be successful in a variety of ways. The appeal of being in Los Angeles was a huge factor for him early on in the recruiting process."

Texas wouldn't offer for another year as the Longhorns were dialed in on a five-star running back in their home state. Galena Park North Shore's Zach Evans was being talked about as a generational prospect, and Tom Herman was all in on him.

Texas offensive coordinator Tim Beck had extensive ties to Arizona. Beck spent time as the head coach at Saguaro High School in the Phoenix area and kept relationships with coaches and players in the state as a recruiter. The Longhorns offered Robinson in January of 2019, and initially he spoke highly of Texas.

"This offer means a lot," Robinson told *247Sports*. "Just to see how good of a program Texas is and to see all the great players that come in and out of there is pretty cool. And talking to the coaches is awesome as well. I talk to Coach Beck all the time—that's who I really talk to a lot. Coach Beck is the man. I love his personality and how outgoing he is. He's a great recruiter and knows how to get players to his school."

A visit materialized quickly, and Robinson was able to make a trip to Austin with several of his coaches and a few teammates. It was on that visit when Texas established itself as a contender. Beck played a huge part in the recruitment, but Robinson really connected with running backs coach Stan Drayton. Robinson has been vocal about his faith and the Christian upbringing he had while he was being raised by his grandparents Cleo and Gerri Robinson. A former Pac-12 official, Cleo played a big role in Robinson's upbringing and served as a mentor on and off the field.

Robinson could have easily chosen USC and stayed out west, but he always expressed a desire to blaze his own trail. Early in his recruitment, schools such as Michigan, Notre Dame, and UCLA seemed to be favorites, but two schools emerged as serious contenders down the stretch. Following a junior season that saw Robinson run for 2,400 yards and 35 touchdowns on a staggering 14.1 yards per carry, he began to start narrowing his choices.

"I think it was a combination of USC and UCLA not performing and other schools became more heavily involved," Angulo said. "Those two schools had offered him early, and he was talking to them consistently. I think he had made it out to USC and UCLA at least three times each, so it was kind of a comfort level with those two schools from a continuity standpoint and developing those relationships. He started to get recruited even more heavily by some other programs, and that opened up the way he was looking and approaching things. There were the SEC schools, Oklahoma, Ohio State, and Texas. A bunch of programs started to get involved and I think that opened up his own net that he was casting in terms of the schools he was considering. He broadened it a bit. I think there were also some miscommunications in terms of USC and UCLA. Both of those schools eased off a little bit, thinking they were going to be involved heavily regardless. Obviously they were still in that final group, but, in a sense, I think they both got caught napping a little bit."

Ohio State was heavily involved for Robinson after making an early offer, but the visit to Texas solidified the Longhorns at the top of his list. In May, sources indicated to *Horns247* that Texas was emerging as a heavy favorite. The Longhorns would host Robinson once again for an official visit in June during their annual "Heat Wave" pool party.

The beginning of the visit almost backfired on the Longhorns. Robinson felt coming in that he was the priority for Texas at running back, but a surprise visit from Evans could have ruined that.

Evans previously cut Texas from his list of top schools, telling *247Sports* that he had major concerns about the Longhorns' future as a championship contender. Then Evans popped up on campus in a quiet manner on the day that Robinson was set to arrive in Austin. There was a lot of concern within the staff, as Evans' visit was orchestrated without the knowledge of the entire staff. There was some tension as the staff split between playing the game with Evans and focusing attention on Robinson.

In the end, it didn't matter. Robinson's visit went off well and there was supreme confidence from the coaching staff coming out of the weekend. Many within the athletic facility were talking as if Robinson were already a member of the class. Ohio State remained the key competition, but Texas was able to get the last official visit. After looking like a lock to stay out west, Robinson was down to two schools outside of the region.

"I think he started to recognize that he could go anywhere and thrive," Angulo said. "It wasn't that he needed USC or UCLA. He didn't need a program to get the best out of him. He was more about going wherever he could to find the best fit in terms of style and in terms of depth chart and in terms of being on the field early and contribute and make an impact. I think he went out to Texas and started to recognize that this was a team he could help turn around and a program he could become a sort of savior for. That was, I think, the biggest appeal for him. I remember catching up with him and hearing him talk about his relationships with the coaches and what they were telling him and what he was looking at in terms of his potential impact. I think it far exceeded what he would be able to do at USC, which already has a really established running back lineage.

UCLA was a new program as well, but he saw Texas as a project he could really embrace and be the cornerstone of."

The following week Robinson flew to Atlanta for the Rivals.com Five-Star Challenge. It was there that rumors of Ohio State surging in his recruitment started to take off. While he was at the camp, Robinson was surrounded by several Ohio State commits, including his high school teammate Lathan Ransom. Robinson would later say that the pressure from the other Buckeyes commits got to him.

"This whole time I knew it was Texas, but all the pressure coming to me from Ohio State was a reason why I was going there initially," Robinson told *247Sports*. "Then I realized that it wasn't for me. Everything that I need is at Texas."

Despite the positive feelings from Texas, Robinson made a silent commitment to Ohio State. At that point, he stopped communicating with the Longhorns. It looked like Texas would miss out on a huge target, and the outlook at the running back position didn't look good. After talking it over and praying over his decision, Robinson decided not to go public with his commitment to Ohio State.

"With Ohio State, I think his best relationship among anyone, with any of the coaches recruiting him, was with Tony Alford," Angulo said. "[Alford] has a lot of ties out west—he played his college ball at Colorado State, and he recruits the West Coast. [Robinson's] relationship with Alford was the big appeal with the Buckeyes. I think there were a lot of things going on there with Ryan Day taking over for Urban Meyer and how things were transitioning for that program as well. That made it one of those things where he could possibly go there and be part of this new wave of Buckeyes. He started to just recognize that there weren't just a couple of schools he could go to and make an impact at. Going out and seeing those places really opened his eyes."

After his recruitment was done, Robinson told reporters his decision was driven by prayer. Other sources indicated his grandparents didn't feel Ohio State was the best choice for him and wanted him closer to home. For the most part, seeing Texas last played a big role.

"He was able to take his officials, and, for the most part, he was a lean to a lot of different schools at different points in the process," Angulo said. "He would go to one school, and he would love it. I think coaches at every stop would feel very comfortable with where they stood with him. It was one of those things where I feel that if the process had stretched out another six or seven months, he would have had a different leader. He went out to Ohio State first, and that was the school that really made a huge impression. He felt he was probably going to go there, and then he had his official visit to USC, and then he had his official visit to Texas. After that Ohio State visit, I caught up with him and got all of his thoughts on Coach Day and the offense and Coach Alford and what they viewed in him. He was considering shutting everything down. For the most part, he had always said that if he found the best fit, he wouldn't wait any longer or hesitate to make a decision. At the time there was another teammate of his, Lathan Ransom, who was also considering Ohio State heavily. He ended up signing there, and the two had talked about potentially teaming up together and playing together and doing all that. Kelee Ringo had also considered Ohio State and Texas. Those three were always in conversation with one another, as far as teaming up and doing something as an Arizona trio at the next stop. He was close to committing to Ohio State. Some would say he silently committed to them before backing off of that and then ultimately committing to Texas after his official visit there. I think you have to tip the hat to whoever at Texas was in charge of scheduling that trip and figuring out that he wanted to commit early and do it before the summer was over. Whoever made sure they were the last official visit got it done. The way those musical chairs played out obviously benefitted the Longhorns."

Robinson also said he felt led to Texas through his prayers to God. Robinson was vocal throughout his recruitment about his faith, and he put his trust in that to make the call.

"I mean, just a lot of prayer," Robinson told *247Sports*. "You know, God kind of led me into [the] decision of me going to Texas, and with Ohio State there was just a lot of people [in] my ear and people telling me that you should go here or you should go here with the class that they got. You know, it sounded real good to me. But what the big picture is and what was really for me is at Texas."

Drayton remained a huge reason why Robinson chose Texas. When Robinson originally informed the staff that he would be heading to Ohio State, Drayton handled it in a way that left the door open for the Longhorns.

"We did a lot with Stan Drayton," Cleo Robinson told *247Sports*. "We drove around with him on campus during our official visit, and my wife confronted him with tough personal questions. He was touched by that and never wavered. He said, 'I never answered questions like that before.' I don't remember the exact questions, but his response was impressive and showed the real person in him."

Cleo would go on to say that when he was told of the Ohio State decision, Drayton voiced nothing but support and told him that it was a pleasure to recruit Robinson. That relationship was the biggest key in the recruitment, as Robinson repeatedly raved about the Texas running backs coach.

"Me and Coach Stan are super close," Robinson told *247Sports*. "It's rare you get a coach who believes in God, and we talk about scripture every day. We send each other a lot of things to motivate the both of us. Coach Drayton—what he's come from and the running backs he's produced in the NFL—he's the best running back coach. He had Zeke [Ezekiel Elliott] and kind of developed him from high school through college. I feel like he's going to do that for me. It's family at Texas, and Coach Drayton is a God-fearing man, and that's good for me because I feel he'd be the best for me in developing as a person. Off the field, he's about staying strong in your faith and being a good man. On the field, he's coached some big-time backs before, like Ezekiel Elliott, Matt Forte, Arian Foster—it's a good look for me."

Angulo feels the biggest factor for Robinson was the opportunity to be a part of rebuilding the program at Texas.

"For him, it was just the opportunity to be a huge impact guy," Angulo said. "He realized he could be the guy who helps bring Texas back. I don't think we could ever downplay the impact that has on a recruit and the way he looks at a school and approaches the process. There are some players who might take the easy way out and go compete for a college football playoff spot at Ohio State or be the next Heisman Trophy running back at USC. I think he saw it as a challenge. That's the biggest thing I took away from the official to Texas. It's obviously closer to home. It's not too far. It's a two-hour-max flight, so his grandparents could go see him. From an impact standpoint, he saw that as the best opportunity to become legendary. He can be a guy who goes and does big things at a school. There's a bigger potential for impact there than any other school, and I think he embraced that."

While many wouldn't want to take on the challenge or miss out on playing for a championship to be part of a rebuild, Robinson was always different. Angulo felt the move was a confidence move to bet on himself.

"He's always been super independent and a self-thinker," Angulo said. "He's a player who oozes a ton of confidence in himself. I think going to Texas was the ultimate bet-on-myself move. He was saying, 'It doesn't matter where I go; I'm going to be Bijan Robinson.' I think he's just been so well taught, and the way he was brought up was so commendable and admirable. You kind of look at his work ethic and his demeanor and the way he's gone about everything, and it's no shock he's had the success he's had at Texas.

"I...remember going out to a spring showcase in the spring before his official visits. In Arizona they do these spring showcases where they bring together four or five schools on one campus, and they invite all the college coaches who are in town that day to go and see multiple teams at once instead of hopping from school to school. I remember we were at Desert Vista High School in southwest Phoenix, and Salpointe Catholic took a bus all the way up to Phoenix to make sure that prospects were able to perform in front of coaches. Despite that two-hour drive from Tucson in late spring, where it gets up to 115°F or so in the afternoon, they broke off, and he went with the running backs to the baseball field on the other side of campus, hauling all of his gear. All the coaches followed him, and you would have thought this was a pro day workout or the NFL Combine. The way he was going about his business and the way he was working out, he could have been lax. He had all the offers at that point. He's the best running back on the West Coast. He was a five-star in my book at that time. He had it all, but the way he was sweating made it seem like he had nothing. That image is what I'll always remember about Bijan as a recruit."

With the big win secured, Texas would go about protecting its prized recruit for the next few months. The Longhorns struggled mightily on the field, and several programs continued to pursue the elite back. Robinson talked of taking other visits several different times, but he never ended up making the trips. At the end of the season, Texas cleaned house and replaced several coaches, including offensive coordinator Tim Beck.

"So I texted him on December 1," Angulo said. "I think the changes had happened and a bunch of schools had already reached out. I know USC had been trying to make a push. UCLA had not gotten an official visit from him, so they were trying to get back into it. He was cordial with a couple of these schools, as he is. He's a well-mannered kid, so he told them thanks but no thanks. I think he had already made up his mind that no matter who the coaches were at Texas, he already had this on his agenda as a thing he wanted to accomplish. That was to help Texas get back on track as a football program. His response to me was, 'Nothing will change for me. I'm still with Texas. I will not be taking any other visits.' He was all in even though there was no concrete info on who the coaches would be—the program itself was already the thing he signed up for, and that wasn't going to change."

Drayton was one of the few assistants retained, and that paid off for Robinson as he continued to believe in his development ability. With the future of the Texas program in question, Robinson began to believe he could be part of the turnaround in Austin.

"That's exactly what I was thinking," Robinson told *247Sports*. "With Coach Drayton as running back coach, he can develop you to be, you know, the best running back you can be. Just how he handled himself as a coach and as a person and the experiences he's had and the players that he's been with and NFL experience—I feel like that was a big reason for me."

Robinson capped his high school career with another sensational season, running for 2,235 yards and 38 touchdowns on 17.7 yards per carry. His 7,036 career yards and 114 career touchdowns both are records for any player in Arizona high school football. Robinson was selected to play in the All-American Bowl and Polynesian Bowl following the season.

"I just think he was remarkable in his ability to make big plays," Angulo said. "He was a home-run threat from anywhere on the field. I loved his vision, and I loved his ability to hit the second level and make a cut up field. I was a little bit concerned about his ball security. At that level of competition, you could probably dance a little bit with the ball and it wouldn't matter. He could kind of do some things and have it out away from his body and wiggle his way through traffic. That was my biggest concern about him going to college, but he's been able to shore that up, and I think his explosiveness was absolutely evident that it would play anywhere. I'd go out and see him and think, 'Could he play in Texas? Could he play in the Trinity League in California? Could he play with some of these better teams?' The answer was always yes. I never had any doubts about his production. If you're going to play against those schools, you have to dominate. He was averaging 20 yards per carry or something crazy like that and just scoring these ridiculous touchdowns. You just knew that once he raised the level of difficulty, he would still be a pretty remarkable player."

Several teams attempted to turn the tide on Robinson down the stretch. Robinson hosted a few schools for in-home visits, and the negative recruiting revved up as coaches aimed to pry Robinson away from Texas. After he signed, Robinson said that stretch was the most stressful time for him.

"Probably the end of the recruitment," Robinson told *247Sports*. "Toward signing day, a lot of coaches, they were trying hard to try and tell you a lot of negative things about other programs. About the people you know. I don't know if it is true or not, but they say a lot of negative things about the program you're going [to] try to get you to go to their program."

Robinson was one of the last signatures to be faxed in on signing day. As fans worried, Robinson simply wanted to wait to sign with the rest of his teammates during a ceremony at Salpointe Catholic in the afternoon. Once Robinson's signature was in, everyone in Austin could breathe easy. Asked if he had any regrets or anything he'd do differently, Robinson stated he was pleased with the process.

"Nothing," Robinson told *247Sports*. "If you have the chance to have that experience, I feel you shouldn't have any regrets through it. But, you know, it is a fun process to go through, for me."

Robinson arrived in Austin in June 2020, during the COVID-19 pandemic. His first season on campus would be one to remember, as the nation tried to work through the deadly pandemic.

As a freshman, Robinson ran for 703 yards and four touchdowns, but he was underutilized until late in the season. Of his 703 yards, 522 came over the final four games of the season, and 355 of those yards came in the final two games of the season.

Following Robinson's freshman year, Herman was fired as the head coach at Texas. Steve Sarkisian's arrival in Austin meant that Robinson would see more of a featured role going forward. As a sophomore, Robinson earned All-Big 12 honors and was named a semifinalist for the Maxwell and Doak Walker Awards.

Robinson led the team in rushing, with 1,127 yards and 11 touchdowns, and he also contributed 26 receptions for 295 yards and four touchdowns. Robinson was injured near the end of the year and missed the final two games of the season as Texas finished a disappointing 5–7 under first-year head coach Steve Sarkisian.

Many anticipate that the 2022 season could be Robinson's final season at Texas. A surefire draft pick, Robinson is expected to bolt for the NFL early, provided he turns in a strong junior campaign. Robinson, a preseason Heisman contender, has already proven to be marketable, cashing in during the first year of the Name, Image, and Likeness (NIL) era.

The NIL rule that was passed by the NCAA to allow players the ability to make money through endorsement deals is still in its infancy. Robinson took advantage early on, partnering with companies such as C4 Energy, Athletic Brewing Company, Raising Cane's, and DAZN.

Because of his popularity, companies are paying a premium for Robinson and other players like him to endorse and promote them on social media. When asked in an ESPN radio interview, Robinson talked more about his experience on the business side of football.

"It's huge. It's a huge blessing. I've learned so much just being around the business, and I'm just learning about different companies," Robinson said. "In the NFL, you deal with them all the time, and with me dealing with this now, it's a cool experiment for all the college athletes that are doing it. But for me and the companies that I'm working with, they reach out to other companies that I'm working with, and then they reach out to me. So it's just great to have those options and just learn about those behind-the-scenes things about what companies are about, how they operate, and what I can do for them. It's been a fun process this whole time. I pray that I get a lot more down the road, but what I have now has been a fun journey, and I just want to keep growing with it."

Robinson also announced a clothing line deal with Centre, a Texas-based apparel company that allowed Robinson to have a hand in designing his own gear.

The book is still being written on Robinson, but Texas will depend heavily on him in 2022. In that same radio interview with ESPN Tucson, Robinson talked more about using his voice as a leader.

"I learned a lot these first two years being a college football player. I know that God gave me a gift, but I learned how to read certain defenses, watch film, grow mentally. At Texas, [running backs coach Stan Drayton] has been a huge help for me, and he's helped out so many guys like Ezekiel Elliott and other big names in the NFL. [Drayton] has taught me so much about being a better leader.

"You know me—I lead by example, and I don't say much, but my voice will be a huge deal for me going into this season. I'm gonna let the guys hear me instead of just watch, and they can get energy off that. I want to use my voice for certain situations and just be more vocal around the whole team."

Robinson is also focused on his own personal development. Drayton is now gone—the coach who was so vital in landing Robinson left Texas during the off-season to take the head coach position at Temple. New running back coach Tashard Choice is a similar man of faith, and Robinson is focused on the bigger picture in 2022.

"I just want to grow in my faith. I've been doing that this whole time. You have individual accolades, but bringing the team together and making the team as strong as it can, whether it's through the transfer portal or through recruits—but I want to make this the strongest team Texas could have. It starts with leadership and being player led, because if your team is doing good, then all the individual accolades will come to you and everyone on the team.

"I just want to be the best leader I can and be the guy on the team that takes this team over the hump. That's my goal for this coming year."

No analyst in the business covered Robinson closer than Angulo. Now that the recruitment is over, and Angulo is watching Robinson's career unfold, he isn't surprised one bit.

"You're talking to the wrong guy," Angulo laughed. "I don't think I was surprised at all. I think I had him ranked the highest out of all the analysts at *247Sports*. We have a feature called 'My Five Stars,' and he was in there early for me when we started to come up with those. I'm never truly surprised by anything he does. He's just that kind of player that when things start to go south, he raises his game up a level. If he's struggling or there's some competition, I think he always finds a different gear to surpass those expectations. He was remarkable this past year [2021], and he heads into this season [2022] as probably one of the better offensive players in the country and a projected first-round draft pick. I think we see how important versatile running backs are in terms of not only being three-down backs but also catching the ball out of the backfield and making defenders miss. They will be able to flex him out in the pro game as well. All of those things he can do—he's showcasing at the college level, and it's going to be fun to track his path as he keeps churning forward."

Acknowledgments

My name might be the only one on the cover, but this book wouldn't be possible without many of the people in my life. My beautiful wife, Kylie, is at the top of that list. That life of a spouse married to a recruiting reporter isn't glamorous. Many times it means weekends alone, vacations in February, Christmas plans pushed back for state championships and signing day, and a constantly distracted husband who can't put his phone down when he's home. It means going to events alone because I'm off on a field somewhere. It means putting everything in her life on hold at a moment's notice to support me.

Through it all, my wife has shown nothing but unwavering support and belief in my ability. Saying I wouldn't be in this position without her isn't just a hollow, feel-good phrase—everything I've done in my career was possible because she first believed I could do it. Throw in the work of writing a book on top of my normal life and it makes double the workload for her to carry. Kylie, thank you for being self-less so I can be selfish. Thank you for shrinking so that I can grow. I don't know that I'll ever be able to pay it back to you.

To my dog, Winston. While my four-legged little buddy didn't directly pen anything in these pages, he kept me company through many late nights as I stressed about finishing the manuscript.

I want to thank my family, starting with my parents, Greg and Mitzi. Both encouraged me at a young age to read, and my father gave me both a love for football and the written word. Thank you for your support. To my nana, who always taught the value of hard work and education and always put up with a hyper kid who had a lot to say.

To my brother and sister-in-law, John and Marie, and my nephew, Conor, I thank you for your belief, encouragement, and love as I embarked on this project. Saturdays in the fall are spent at their house watching Texas football. You are our best friends.

I also want to thank my friends of whom there are way too many to name. While many people surround themselves with others who ask, 'Why?' I've found a group of people who ask, 'Why not?' Be it my lifelong best friends or my professional friends who make up my network, each and every one of you has a place in my heart.

My talented coworker Jeff Howe was originally set to coauthor this book but decided he couldn't commit the time to the project. Despite that, Jeff was integral behind the scenes, helping to advise me in the right directions and helping me get access to players and coaches. He was the one person besides my wife who saw this project take shape behind the scenes.

Thank you to E.J. Holland and Bobby Burton, who saw promise in me as a raw reporter trying to work his way up and took a chance bringing me to *Horns247*.

Thank you to Josh Williams and Triumph Books for making this possible. I never imagined I'd be able to author a book, but they believed enough in me to choose me for the project.

To my editor, Jeff Fedotin, thank you for walking me through the process, editing all of my mistakes, and generally just keeping me calm as I dove into something I'd never done before.

None of this would be possible without the players and coaches I spoke with to put this book together. To the former Texas players Blake Brockermeyer, Quan Cosby, B.J. Johnson, Derrick Johnson, Fozzy Whittaker, Roy Miller, Rod Wright, Michael Huff, Rod Babers, and Aaron Williams, and to Blair Angulo of *247Sports* who helped me greatly throughout Bijan Robinson's recruitment and again in this book.

Walking down memory lane with many of these huge names was so much fun. It reminded me of what Texas football once was and what it could be again. Through this process, I was able to forge new friendships and lean on old ones with these players to get this done. Thank you for accepting the invitation to join me in this and for opening up in unimaginable ways during our conversations.

Finally, thank you to the Texas Longhorn fans out there who support my work daily and allow me to have this dream job. Sometimes we argue and sometimes I write things they may not like, but they make my life possible. I hope you enjoy this book, and perhaps we will do another volume in the future. Hook 'Em.

Sources

Austin American-Statesman
Dallas Morning News
ESPN Radio Tucson
Houston Chronicle
Longhorn Network
Pro-Football-Reference.com
Sports-Reference.com
TexasSports.com
Tucson.com
247Sports.com